Cisco Networking Academy Program

IT Essentials I: PC Hardware and Software Engineering Journal and Workbook

Cisco Systems, Inc.
Cisco Networking Academy Program

Cisco Press

201 West 103rd Street
Indianapolis, IN 46290 USA

Cisco Networking Academy Program
IT Essentials I:
PC Hardware and Software Engineering Journal and Workbook

Cisco Systems, Inc.
Cisco Networking Academy Program

Course Sponsored by Hewlett-Packard Company

Copyright © 2003 Cisco Systems, Inc.

Published by:
Cisco Press
210 West 103rd Street
Indianapolis, IN 46290 USA

All rights reserved. No part of this book may be reproduced or transmitted in any form or by any means electronic or mechanical, including photocopying, recording, or by any information storage and retrieval system, without written permission from the publisher, except for the inclusion of brief quotations in a review.

Printed in the United States of America   1 2 3 4 5 6 7 8 9 0

First Printing   January 2003

ISBN: 1-58713-093-9

Warning and Disclaimer

This book is designed to provide information about PC hardware and software setup, configuration, and troubleshooting. Every effort has been made to make this book as complete and as accurate as possible, but no warranty or fitness is implied.

The information is provided on an "as is" basis. The author, Cisco Press, and Cisco Systems, Inc. shall have neither liability nor responsibility to any person or entity with respect to any loss or damages arising from the information contained in this book or from the use of the programs that may accompany it.

The opinions expressed in this book belong to the author and are not necessarily those of Cisco Systems, Inc.

 This book is part of the Cisco Networking Academy Program series from Cisco Press. The products in this series support and complement the Cisco Networking Academy Program curriculum. If you are using this book outside the Networking Academy program, then you are not preparing with a Cisco trained and authorized Networking Academy provider.

For information on the Cisco Networking Academy Program or to locate a Networking Academy, please visit www.cisco.com/edu.

Trademark Acknowledgments

All terms mentioned in this book that are known to be trademarks or service marks have been appropriately capitalized. Cisco Press or Cisco Systems, Inc., cannot attest to the accuracy of this information. Use of a term in this book should not be regarded as affecting the validity of any trademark or service mark.

The logo of the CompTIA Authorized Curriculum Program and the status of this or other training material as "Authorized" under the CompTIA Authorized Curriculum Program signifies that, in CompTIA's opinion, such training material covers the content of the CompTIA's related certification exam. CompTIA has not reviewed or approved the accuracy of the contents of this training material and specifically disclaims any warranties of merchantability or fitness for a particular purpose. CompTIA makes no guarantee concerning the success of persons using any such "Authorized" or other training material in order to prepare for any CompTIA certification exam.

Feedback Information

At Cisco Press, our goal is to create in-depth technical books of the highest quality and value. Each book is crafted with care and precision, undergoing rigorous development that involves the unique expertise of members of the professional technical community.

Readers' feedback is a natural continuation of this process. If you have any comments regarding how we could improve the quality of this book, or otherwise alter it to better suit your needs, you can contact us at networkingacademy@ciscopress.com. Please be sure to include the book title and ISBN in your message.

We greatly appreciate your assistance.

Publisher	John Wait
Editor-in-Chief	John Kane
Executive Editor	Carl Lindholm
Cisco Representative	Anthony Wolfenden
Cisco Press Program Manager	Sonia Torres Chavez
Cisco Marketing Communications Manager	Tom Geitner
Cisco Marketing Program Manager	Edie Quiroz
Production Manager	Patrick Kanouse
Development Editor	Deborah Doorley
Senior Editor	Sheri Cain
Technical Editors	Jim Drennen, Arthur Toch, Arthur Tucker
Copy Editor	Cris Mattison

CISCO SYSTEMS

Corporate Headquarters
Cisco Systems, Inc.
170 West Tasman Drive
San Jose, CA 95134-1706
USA
http://www.cisco.com
Tel: 408 526-4000
    800 553-NETS (6387)
Fax: 408 526-4100

European Headquarters
Cisco Systems Europe
11 Rue Camille Desmoulins
92782 Issy-les-Moulineaux
Cedex 9
France
http://www-europe.cisco.com
Tel: 33 1 58 04 60 00
Fax: 33 1 58 04 61 00

Americas Headquarters
Cisco Systems, Inc.
170 West Tasman Drive
San Jose, CA 95134-1706
USA
http://www.cisco.com
Tel: 408 526-7660
Fax: 408 527-0883

Asia Pacific Headquarters
Cisco Systems Australia,
Pty., Ltd
Level 17, 99 Walker Street
North Sydney
NSW 2059 Australia
http://www.cisco.com
Tel: +61 2 8448 7100
Fax: +61 2 9957 4350

Cisco Systems has more than 200 offices in the following countries. Addresses, phone numbers, and fax numbers are listed on the Cisco Web site at www.cisco.com/go/offices

Argentina • Australia • Austria • Belgium • Brazil • Bulgaria • Canada • Chile • China • Colombia • Costa Rica • Croatia • Czech Republic • Denmark • Dubai, UAE • Finland • France • Germany • Greece • Hong Kong • Hungary • India • Indonesia • Ireland Israel • Italy • Japan • Korea • Luxembourg • Malaysia • Mexico • The Netherlands • New Zealand • Norway • Peru • Philippines Poland • Portugal • Puerto Rico • Romania • Russia • Saudi Arabia • Scotland • Singapore • Slovakia • Slovenia • South Africa • Spain Sweden • Switzerland • Taiwan • Thailand • Turkey • Ukraine • United Kingdom • United States • Venezuela • Vietnam • Zimbabwe

Copyright © 2000, Cisco Systems, Inc. All rights reserved. Access Registrar, AccessPath, Are You Ready, ATM Director, Browse with Me, CCDA, CCDE, CCDP, CCIE, CCNA, CCNP, CCSI, CD-PAC, CiscoLink, the Cisco NetWorks logo, the Cisco Powered Network logo, Cisco Systems Networking Academy, Fast Step, FireRunner, Follow Me Browsing, FormShare, GigaStack, IGX, Intelligence in the Optical Core, Internet Quotient, IP/VC, iQ Breakthrough, iQ Expertise, iQ FastTrack, iQuick Study, iQ Readiness Scorecard, The iQ Logo, Kernel Proxy, MGX, Natural Network Viewer, Network Registrar, the Networkers logo, Packet, PIX, Point and Click Internetworking, Policy Builder, RateMUX, ReyMaster, ReyView, ScriptShare, Secure Script, Shop with Me, SlideCast, SMARTnet, SVX, TrafficDirector, TransPath, VlanDirector, Voice LAN, Wavelength Router, Workgroup Director, and Workgroup Stack are trademarks of Cisco Systems, Inc.; Changing the Way We Work, Live, Play, and Learn, Empowering the Internet Generation, are service marks of Cisco Systems, Inc.; and Aironet, ASIST, BPX, Catalyst, Cisco, the Cisco Certified Internetwork Expert Logo, Cisco IOS, the Cisco IOS logo, Cisco Press, Cisco Systems, Cisco Systems Capital, the Cisco Systems logo, Collision Free, Enterprise/Solver, EtherChannel, EtherSwitch, FastHub, FastLink, FastPAD, IOS, IP/TV, IPX, LightStream, LightSwitch, MICA, NetRanger, Post-Routing, Pre-Routing, Registrar, StrataView Plus, Stratm, SwitchProbe, TeleRouter, are registered trademarks of Cisco Systems, Inc. or its affiliates in the U.S. and certain other countries.

All other brands, names, or trademarks mentioned in this document or Web site are the property of their respective owners. The use of the word partner does not imply a partnership relationship between Cisco and any other company. (0010R)

Table of Contents

Introduction

The CISCO NETWORKING ACADEMY PROGRAM IT Essentials I: PC Hardware and Software Engineering Journal and Workbook supplements the online course and the companion guide. The Engineering Journal and Workbook summarizes the material to focus on the details of hardware components and software. By doing the research required, you will become thoroughly knowledgeable of the concepts.

Completing the journal allows you to develop and express a clear understanding of the topics covered. It also provides the competencies when the goal is to pass the A+ Certification and to continue with IT Essentials II: Network Operating Systems.

The topics covered in the book include the internal components of a computer used to successfully assemble a system, installing an operating system, and troubleshooting using system tools and diagnostic software. In addition, you will work with architectures to connect to the Internet and to share resources in a network environment.

You will find that your studies are best complemented by a text that describes the theory and foundational concepts found in the Engineering Journal. To that end, Cisco Press offers CISCO NETWORKING ACADEMY PROGRAM IT Essentials I: PC Hardware and Software Companion Guide, which includes thorough treatments of the topics discussed in this journal. In addition, the IT Essentials I: PC Hardware and Software Lab Companion provides the hands-on experience that allows you to apply your knowledge to exercises with the components and software studied in the course.

Who Should Read This Book

This book is intended for the student in high school, technical school, community college, or a four-year institution who wants to pursue a career in IT technology or who wants to have working knowledge of how a computer works, how to assemble a computer, and how to troubleshoot hardware and software issues.

This Book's Organization

This book is divided into chapters that correspond to the chapters in the companion guide.

- Chapter 1, "Information Technology Basics"—This chapter focuses on Windows basics, number conversions that include binary, decimal, and hexadecimal, and lab safety.

- Chapter 2, "How Computers Work"—Internal components of a computer are covered in this chapter that include the motherboard, ROM and BIOS chips, video card, and the power supply.

- Chapter 3, "Computer Assembly"—This chapter focuses on assembling a computer system and connecting the power supply, motherboard, and drives.

- Chapter 4, "Operating System Fundamentals"—Operating system fundamentals and navigation is covered in this chapter. The focus is on DOS, DOS commands, and creating a boot disk.

- Chapter 5, "Windows 9x Operating Systems"—The focus of this chapter is the operating system and installing Windows 98. This includes navigating the Desktop, the file structure, and the file management system Troubleshooting skills include installing drivers and creating a Windows startup disk.

- Chapter 6, "PC Multimedia"—This chapter covers multimedia including both sound and video. You will install a sound card and update the video card, plus learn the terminology as it relates to CDs and DVDs.

- Chapter 7, "Windows NT/2000/XP Operating Systems"—The differences between Windows 9x and Windows 2000 are detailed in this chapter. You will upgrade from Windows 98 to Windows 2000 and create an emergency startup disk.

- Chapter 8, "Advanced Hardware Fundamentals for Servers"—This chapter covers the concepts and configurations of RAID, the steps to add a processor to a server, and how to upgrade a server adapter.

- Chapter 9, "Networking Fundamentals"—Networking is detailed in this chapter including the types of networks, topology, and connecting to the Internet. The network interface card (NIC) is installed and configured, plus you will troubleshoot using the PING command.

- Chapter 10, "Printers"—In this chapter, you will learn general printer maintenance, manage files in a printer queue, and allow print sharing.

- Chapter 11, "Preventive Maintenance"—In this chapter, the focus is on preventive maintenance including using a digital multimeter, cleaning computer components, and using system tools. Environmental issues, ESD, and general preventive maintenance are covered.

- Chapter 12, "Troubleshooting Hardware"—Troubleshooting basics are covered in this chapter. The steps of the troubleshooting cycle and identifying POST errors are discussed. Additionally, troubleshooting printers and hardware in general is covered.

- Chapter 13, "Troubleshooting Software"—Troubleshooting, as it relates to software, is the focus of this chapter. You will boot to the Safe Mode, use the Windows 2000 Recovery Console, and back up the Windows Registry.

This Book's Features

This book contains several elements that help you learn about the basics of hardware and software for the PC:

- **Concept Question**—Each chapter includes a concept question that tests your knowledge of the material. Concept questions range from real-life scenarios to reflective ideas where the answers are not always obvious.

- **Review Questions**—To demonstrate an understanding of the concepts covered, review questions are included that strengthen your understanding. These questions help validate your comprehension of the material covered.

The conventions used to present command syntax in this book are the same conventions used in the *Cisco IOS Command Reference*:

- **Bold** indicates commands and keywords that are entered literally as shown. In examples (not syntax), bold indicates user input (for example, a **show** command).

- *Italic* indicates arguments for which you supply values.

- Braces ({ }) indicate a required element.

- Square brackets ([ ]) indicate an optional element.

- Vertical bars (|) separate alternative, mutually exclusive elements.

- Braces and vertical bars within square brackets (such as [x {y | z}]) indicate a required choice within an optional element. You do not need to enter what is in the brackets, but if you do, you have some required choices in the braces.

CompTIA Authorized Quality Curriculum

The contents of this training material were created for the CompTIA A+ Certification exam covering CompTIA certification exam objectives that were current as of December 2002.

How to Become CompTIA Certified

This training material can help you prepare for and pass a related CompTIA certification exam or exams. In order to achieve CompTIA certification, you must register for and pass a CompTIA certification exam or exams.

In order to become CompTIA certified, you must:

1. Select a certification exam provider. For more information please visit http://www.comptia.org/certification/general_information/test_locations.asp
2. Register for and schedule a time to take the CompTIA certification exam(s) at a convenient location.
3. Read and sign the Candidate Agreement, which will be presented at the time of the exam(s). The text of the Candidate Agreement can be found at http://www.comptia.org/certification/general_information/candidate_agreement.asp
4. Take and pass the CompTIA certification exam(s).

For more information about CompTIA's certifications, such as their industry acceptance, benefits, or program news, please visit http://www.comptia.org/certification/default.asp

CompTIA is a non-profit information technology (IT) trade association. CompTIA's certifications are designed by subject matter experts from across the IT industry. Each CompTIA certification is vendor-neutral, covers multiple technologies, and requires demonstration of skills and knowledge widely sought after by the IT industry.

To contact CompTIA with any questions or comments:

Please call + 1 630 268 1818

questions@comptia.org

Chapter 1

Information Technology Basics

A computer system consists of hardware and software components. Hardware is the physical equipment such as the case, floppy disk drives, keyboard, monitor, cables, speakers, and printers. The term software describes the programs that operate the computer system. Computer software, or programs, instructs the computer how to operate. These operations can include identifying, accessing, and processing information.

Essentially, a program is a sequence of instructions that describe how data is to be processed. Programs vary widely, depending on the type of information that is to be accessed or generated. For example, the instructions involved in balancing a checkbook are different from those required to simulate a virtual reality world on the Internet.

A group of computers that are connected to share resources are called a network. Businesses, schools, and even home computers can be networked to share files and devices such as printers. Networks can connect computers in a building, a city, and across a continent. The ultimate network is the Internet.

In the 1960s, the U.S. Department of Defense (DoD) recognized the need to establish communication links between major U.S. military installations. Other highlights include the following:

- In 1968, the Advanced Research Projects Agency (ARPA) contracted with a private company, Bolt, Beranek, and Newman, Inc., to build a network based on the packet switching technology that had been developed for better transmission of computer data.

- Throughout the 70s, more nodes or points of access were added both domestically and abroad.

- The Domain Name System (DNS) was introduced in the 80s as a way to map host names to IP addresses, which was an important development considering hosts on the network grew from 10,000 in 1987 to 100,000 in 1989.

- By 1992, more than 1 million hosts existed on the Internet, and the Internet Society (ISOC) was formed.

- Online advertising was big business by 1995, and it continues to grow. Online banking, travel arrangements, and even ordering pizza is possible on the Internet as the global market is targeted.

The Internet continues to grow and major developments occurr almost daily.

This course provides the basics for one of the most exciting careers today. Information Technology (IT) deals with the latest computer technology and connects students, home users, and businesses. The most important concept to learn is safety. Follow the guidelines to create a safe and efficient work environment.

IT Basics

There are two types of software: operating systems and applications. Explain the difference between the two types and list examples of applications used today.

_____
_____
_____
_____

Operating systems are platform specific. Explain what that means.

_____
_____
_____
_____

There are two types of computers: Mainframes and PCs. List advantages and disadvantages for both.

Mainframe Advantages	PC Advantages
Mainframe Disadvantages	**PC Disadvantages**

Starting the computer with the power button is referred to as a _____ boot.

Re-starting the computer is referred to as a _____ boot.

Describe the proper way to shut down Windows and why it is important?

_____

_____

_____

_____

Icons are shortcuts to programs or files that are used in navigation. Explain how to create a shortcut icon in Windows.

_____

_____

_____

_____

Display properties select or adjust the background, screen saver, appearance (including text size), Web (not available in Windows 95), and effects that can be set for the Desktop. List two ways to access the display properties.

_____

_____

_____

_____

Explain how to find system information on a computer running Windows.

_____

_____

_____

_____

Vocabulary

Define the following terms as completely as you can. Use the online Chapter 1 or IT Essentials 1 for help.

Asynchronous

_____

_____

_____

Bit

_____

_____

_____

Byte

_____
_____
_____

Hertz

_____
_____
_____

Kilobit

_____
_____
_____

Kilobyte

_____
_____
_____

Megabit

_____
_____
_____

Megabyte

_____
_____
_____

Nibble

_____
_____
_____

Math for the Digital Age

Computers are built from various types of electronic circuits. These circuits depend on logic gates. There are three primary logic functions: AND, OR, NOT. Read the following action and enter the correct gate. Refer to Appendix B for additional information:

If either input is on, the output is on.

_____

If either input is off, the output is off.

_____

If the input is on, the output is off (and vice versa).

_____

The NOR gate is a combination of what two gates?

_____

Number Systems

Contrast and compare decimal, binary, and hexadecimal numbering systems.

_____
_____
_____
_____

Explain how binary and hexadecimal numbers are used with computers.

_____
_____
_____
_____

Without using a calculator, convert the binary numbers into decimal numbers.

A. 01111011 _____   B. 00000111 _____

C. 11110000 _____   D. 10101010 _____

E. 01010101 _____   F. 10010011 _____

Convert the decimal numbers into binary numbers.

A. 23 _____   B. 131 _____

C. 3 _____   D. 234 _____

Convert the decimal numbers into hexadecimal numbers.

A. 16 _____   B. 131 _____

C. 3 _____   D. 234 _____

Convert the hexadecimal numbers into decimal numbers.

A. 27 _____   B. AA _____

C. 3 _____   D. F1 _____

Safety Requirements

Review Appendix C for the basic lab safety principles, workspace organizational aids, and the lab safety agreement. Safety is a high priority and the guidelines must be followed.

What does ESD stand for? Explain how it can damage computer components.

_____
_____
_____
_____

Describe the tools that can eliminate the danger caused by ESD.

_____
_____
_____
_____

When should a wrist strap not be used for grounding?

_____
_____
_____
_____

When computer systems are partially operable, diagnostic software conducts general system testing. Testing software is usually available on floppy disk.

List the three types of disk software that should be kept in the workspace.

_____
_____
_____

Additional Notes

_____
_____
_____
_____
_____
_____
_____
_____
_____
_____
_____
_____
_____
_____
_____
_____

Labs and Worksheets

The following labs and worksheets are available in *CISCO NETWORKING ACADEMY PROGRAM IT Essentials I: PC Hardware and Software Lab Companion* and as part of the online curriculum. Labs and worksheets are an excellent tool that you can use to help reinforce the material covered in this chapter.

Labs:

1.3.8   Getting to Know Windows

1.5.3   Boolean Operations

1.5.9   Converting Numbers Overview

Worksheets:

1.3.8   Windows Navigation and Settings

1.5.9   Number Systems Exercises

1.6.6   Lab Safety Checklist

A+ Exam Review Questions

The following are review questions for the A+ exam. Answers are found in Appendix A.

1.   The Internet began as a way to?
   a.   Encourage commerce
   b.   Establish communication links between major U.S. military installations
   c.   Regulate discussions between universities
   d.   Distribute advertising

2.   What type of interface is Windows 98?
   a.   Graphical hardware system
   b.   Extended DOS operating system
   c.   Graphical user interface
   d.   File allocation system

3.   What is a group of computers that are connected so that their resources can be shared?
   a.   Network
   b.   Workstation
   c.   Personal Computer
   d.   Internet

4.   In Windows 98, how do you change the icon for an object?
   a.   Highlight the object, click **Start**, and choose **Change Icon**
   b.   Highlight the object, open **My Computer**, and choose **Change Icon**
   c.   Right-click **Properties >Short-Cut tab > Change Icon button**
   d.   Right-click **Properties** > **Change Icon** > **Change**

5.   How do you change display settings in Windows 98?
   a.   Right-click **Desktop > Properties > Settings**
   b.   Right-click **My Computer** > **Properties**
   c.   Click **Start >Settings >Video**
   d.   Click **Start** > **Video** > **Settings**

6. In Windows 98, how is a shortcut created?

    a.   Go to **Start** > **Control Panel** > **Create Shortcut**

    b.   Go to **Start** > **Control Panel** > **Settings** > **Shortcut**

    c.   Right-click the **Desktop** and select **New** > **Shortcut**

    d.   Right-click **Start** and select **New** > **Shortcut**

7. What is the maximum number of characters that a Windows 98 file name is allowed?

    a.   31

    b.   63

    c.   127

    d.   255

8. To find out the version of Windows 98 that is running:

    a.   Boot the computer and watch for the Windows 98 window

    b.   Click **Start** > **Help** > **About**

    c.   Right-click **My Computer** and select **Properties**

    d.   Type **Help** at the MS-DOS command prompt

9. How do you view the file or folder properties in Windows 98?

    a.   Click the icon on the Desktop and select **Properties**

    b.   Right-click the icon on the desktop or in Explorer and select **Properties**

    c.   Drag and drop the icon onto the taskbar

    d.   Go to **Start** > **Properties** > **Files**

10. When you click the Start button in Windows 98, what is not shown?

    a.   Programs

    b.   Help

    c.   Run

    d.   Explorer

11. What is not contained in the Windows 98 Recycle Folder?

    a.   Deleted files

    b.   Deleted folders

    c.   Deleted objects

    d.   Deleted network identification parameters

12. Traditional telephone lines transmit voice over copper wires using?
    a.   Digital signals
    b.   Analog signals
    c.   Electronic signals
    d.   Power signals

13. The decimal or base-10 number system uses?
    a.   8 digits
    b.   12 digits
    c.   10 digits
    d.   5 digits

14. The binary or base-2 number system uses two digits to express all numerical quantities. They are?
    a.   1 and 2
    b.   0 and 2
    c.   3 and 4
    d.   0 and 1

15. Hexadecimal is also known as?
    a.   Base-16 mathematics
    b.   Base-2 mathematics
    c.   Binary mathematics
    d.   Hex numbering scheme

16. Algorithms are?
    a.   Step by step procedures that perform a specific task
    b.   Lists of computer form factors
    c.   An explanation of an analog phone
    d.   Presentation graphics

17. Damage from ESD is most likely to occur when you are?
    a.   Working on a rubber mat
    b.   Using a multimeter on a computer
    c.   Not properly grounded
    d.   Too close to the power unit while it is operating

18. To prevent failures and extend the life of a computer system, you should?
    a. Schedule regular maintenance
    b. Update software when convenient
    c. Maintain a library of technical books
    d. Move the system frequently

19. You should always ground a wrist strap to?
    a. The computer frame
    b. Anything around that is metal
    c. The power supply
    d. An outlet

20. What should you *never* use to remove residues that stick to circuit boards?
    a. Canned air
    b. Rubbing alcohol or isopropyl alcohol
    c. Water
    d. A dry cloth

Chapter 2

How Computers Work

This chapter focuses on the components of the computer. Knowing how each of the components in the computer work together provides the technician the ability to assemble and repair a computer.

Each step that a computer goes through when it is turned on or booted up is critical to the operation of the computer. If one step fails to initialize, the system will not perform normally or might not function at all. The boot process includes the following:

- Initializing and testing

- Loading the operating system

- Boot sequence

It is important for the IT technician to understand the boot process to troubleshoot when problems occur.

The operating system (OS) is a vital part of the computer. It is the software that controls the functionality and provides lower-level routines for applications and programs. Most operating systems provide functions to read and write data on files. It then translates requests for operations on files into operations that the disk controller can carry out. The operating system helps the computer perform four basic operations:

- Input

- Processing

- Output

- Storage

Opening a web page, an e-mail file, or a file from the network are ways to input data. What is the most common way to input data into a computer? _____

After data has been input, the computer can process the data. Processing data usually results in some kind of output. The most common ways to output data is to send it the computer's _____ or _____.

Data storage is one of the most important of the four basic functions of the operating system. The most common way to store data or a file is on the computer's _____.

Initializing and Testing the System Hardware

For an operating system to run, it must be loaded into the computer's random-access memory (RAM). When the computer is first turned on, it launches a small program called the bootstrap loader.

Where is the bootstrap located? _____

Describe the primary function of the bootstrap loader:

_____

_____

_____

_____

_____

_____

To test the computer's hardware, the bootstrap program runs a program called power-on self test (POST) or. In this test, the computer's central processing unit (CPU) checks itself first and then checks the computer's system timer. The POST checks the RAM by writing data to each RAM chip and then reading that data. Any difference indicates a problem.

If the POST finds errors, it sends a message to the computer monitor. If the POST finds errors that cannot be displayed on the monitor, it sends errors in the form of beeps. The POST sends one beep and the screen begins to display OS loading messages after the bootstrap has determined that the computer has passed the POST.

The meaning of any beep code depends on the manufacturer of the Basic Input/Output System (BIOS). There are three major manufacturers of BIOS chips: AMIBIOS (American Megatrends, Inc.), PhoenixBIOS (Phoenix Technologies Ltd), and AwardBIOS (Award Software, Inc.).

Research the BIOS chip in the lab computer. Who is the manufacturer? _____

_____

Using the manufacturer's manual or the Internet, attach a copy of the beep code that applies to the BIOS chip in the lab computer.

_____

_____

The next step for the bootstrap program is to locate the OS and copy it to the computer's RAM. The order in which the bootstrap program searches the OS boot up file can be changed in the system BIOS setup. The most common search order is as follows:

1. _____

_____

2. _____
_____

3. _____
_____

Hardware Components and Vocabulary

Describe at least three of the main considerations when selecting a computer case:

1. _____
_____

2. _____
_____

3. _____
_____

Provide a brief description for the following terms:

Power Supply:_____
_____
_____

Motherboard:_____
_____
_____

Chipset:_____
_____
_____

CPU:_____
_____
_____

Control Unit:_____
_____
_____

Arithmetic/Logic Unit (ALU):_____
_____
_____

Zero-insertion force (ZIF):_____
_____
_____

BIOS :_____
_____

Erasable programmable read-only memory (EPROM):_____
_____
_____

Electrically erasable programmable read-only memory (EEPROM):_____
_____
_____
_____

Flash ROM:_____
_____
_____

Expansion slots are also known as sockets. Common expansion slots are listed below. Indicate the company that developed each and supply a short description.

Industry Standard Architecture (ISA)

_____
_____
_____

Peripheral Component Interconnect (PCI)

_____
_____
_____

Accelerated Graphics Port (AGP)

_____
_____
_____

All the basic components of the computer are connected together by a communication path that is referred to as a bus. The system bus is a parallel collection of conductors that carry data and control signals from one component to another. The three major system bus types are listed below. Provide a brief description of each.

Address Bus

_____
_____
_____

Data Bus

_____
_____
_____

Control Bus

_____
_____
_____

All peripheral devices that connect to the computer such as printers, scanners, and so on, use connectors on the back of the computer known as Input/Output (I/O) ports. An I/O port is a pathway into and out of the computer. Different types of ports on the computer serve different purposes.

Explain the following types of ports:

Serial Port

_____
_____
_____

Parallel Ports

_____
_____
_____

Universal Serial Bus (USB)

_____
_____
_____

FireWire

_____
_____
_____

Integrated Drive Electronics (IDE)

_____

_____

_____

Enhanced IDE

_____

_____

_____

Small Computer System Interface (SCSI)

_____

_____

_____

SCSI devices are typically connected in a series that forms a chain, known as a daisy chain. Because of this, termination is important. Explain the three types of SCSI termination:

1. _____

_____

_____

_____

2. _____

_____

_____

_____

3. _____

_____

_____

_____

RAM is memory that stores frequently used data for rapid retrieval by the processor. It is temporary or volatile memory. Describe the two classes of RAM that are commonly used:

1. _____

_____

_____

_____

2. _____
_____
_____
_____

Define the following:

SRAM:_____
_____

DRAM:_____
_____

SIMM:_____
_____

DIMM:_____
_____

VRAM:_____
_____

WRAM:_____
_____

RAMDAC:_____
_____

Cache Memory:_____
_____

A high quality monitor and a high quality video card are required for both a high resolution and a high refresh rate. Define the following key terms:

Pixels:_____
_____

Refresh Rate:_____
_____

Resolution:_____
_____

Video Memory:_____
_____

AGP Port:_____
_____

The computer's main storage medium is the hard disk drive (HDD). List the components of the HDD and briefly explain the function of each component:

_____
_____
_____
_____
_____
_____
_____
_____
_____
_____
_____
_____
_____

CD technology has evolved from an audio medium to a main component in almost every computer system today. Define the following:

CD-ROM:_____
_____

CD-R:_____
_____

CD-RW:_____
_____

DVD-ROM:_____
_____

Explain the difference between magnetic media and optical media.

_____
_____
_____
_____

Modem is an acronym for what?

_____

Define the function of a modem.

_____
_____
_____
_____

What does UART stand for and what does it do?

_____
_____
_____
_____

Define the function of a network interface card (NIC)

_____
_____
_____
_____

Portable computers are designed to be lightweight and easy to use anywhere. Describe the components that make this possible.

_____
_____
_____
_____
_____
_____
_____
_____
_____
_____

Concept Question

In 1981, Bill Gates said, "640K ought to be enough for anybody." Today, a 100 GB hard drive is available and cable modems provide high-speed Internet connections. In the space below, make some predictions for the future of computer components.

_____
_____
_____
_____
_____
_____
_____
_____
_____
_____
_____
_____
_____
_____
_____
_____

Additional Notes

_____
_____
_____
_____
_____
_____
_____
_____
_____
_____
_____
_____
_____
_____
_____
_____
_____
_____
_____

Labs and Worksheets

The following labs and worksheets are available in *CISCO NETWORKING ACADEMY PROGRAM IT Essentials I: PC Hardware and Software Lab Companion* and as part of the online curriculum. Labs and worksheets are an excellent tool that you can use to help reinforce the material covered in this chapter.

Labs:

2.3.2	Motherboard Identification
2.3.4	Identify ROM and BIOS Chips
2.3.5	Identifying Computer Expansion Slots
2.3.7	Identifying RAM and RAM Sockets
2.3.9	Video Card Identification

Worksheets:

2.3.1	PC Power Supply
2.3.4	BIOS/ROM
2.3.5	Expansion Slots
2.3.7	RAM and RAM Sockets
2.3.9	Video Card
2.3.13	Floppy Drive
2.3.14	Hard Drive Identification
2.3.15	CD-ROM Identification

A+ Exam Review Questions

The following are review questions for the A+ exam. Answers are found in Appendix A.

1.	A bootstrap program that tests the computer's hardware when the system is powered up is called?
	a.	Power-on self test (POST)

	b.	Power-off self test (POST)

	c.	DOS

	d.	HIMEM.SYS

2.	If the POST finds any errors during its routine, it
	a.	Shuts down

	b.	Runs diagnostic software

	c.	Sends a message to the monitor

	d.	Re-boots

3.	What computer component is NOT tested by the POST routine?
	a.	RAM

	b.	Power supply

	c.	Mainboard

	d.	BIOS

4.	 The order in which the bootstrap program searches the OS boot up file can be changed in the?
	a.	System CMOS

	b.	System BIOS

	c.	POST

	d.	Operating System

5.	PC power supplies use?
	a.	Direct Current (DC)

	b.	Voltage

	c.	Alternating Current (AC)

	d.	Amps

6. The temperature of the power supply is controlled by the?
   a. Thermostat
   b. Case cooler
   c. Cooling fan
   d. CPU

7. How do you prevent a power supply from overheating?
   a. Turn down the air conditioner
   b. Verify the vents used for cooling are not blocked
   c. Turn off the computer every night
   d. Disconnect any device not currently in use

8. The main circuit board in a computer is the?
   a. PCI board
   b. Processor board
   c. Memory board
   d. System board or Motherboard

9. Which of the following is not a CPU manufacturer?
   a. Intel
   b. Cyrex
   c. Sun Microsystems
   d. Advanced Micro Devices

10. When the computer is first turned on, it launches a program called?
    a. CPU
    b. RAM
    c. Bootstrap loader
    d. Cache

11. Pentium CPUs normally run at what voltage?
    a. 3.3 VDC
    b. 12 VDC
    c. 5 VDC
    d. 3 VDC

12. In general, to improve CPU access time, you need to upgrade the?
   a.   Hard drive
   b.   Motherboard
   c.   ROM memory
   d.   Cache

13. BIOS stands for?
   a.   Beginning Information Organization Service
   b.   Basic Input/Output System
   c.   Basic Input/Output Service
   d.   Beginning Information

14. What is the advantage of using flash ROM?
   a.   BIOS can be upgraded without replacing the chip
   b.   The ROM is flashed with new programs every time the system is started
   c.   Hard drives run faster
   d.   Memory is doubled

15. The typical size of a SIMM is?
   a.   32 and 70 pins
   b.   30 and 70 pins
   c.   30 and 72 pins
   d.   32 and 72 pins

16. What type of connector is used for a serial port connection on a PC?
   a.   DB-15, male D-shell
   b.   DB-25, male D-shell
   c.   DB-9, male D-shell
   d.   5-pin, male DIN

17. Hardware resource conflicts are more likely to be IRQ related than I/O related because?
   a.   There are more I/O addresses than IRQs
   b.   BIOS can't control IRQs
   c.   I/O addresses never conflict
   d.   Software corrects I/O conflicts

18. What is a feature of EIDE?
   a. More drives
   b. SCSI connectors
   c. High-speed floppy drives
   d. ATAPI

19. A common failure with SCSI devices is?
   a. Improper termination
   b. Bad terminator
   c. Bad device
   d. Bad Host Adapter

20. What type of interface has the fastest data transfer?
   a. IDE
   b. SCSI
   c. Parallel
   d. Modem

21. The minimum storage unit for an IDE hard drive is called a
   a. Cluster
   b. Cylinder
   c. Byte
   d. Sector

22. The typical CD-ROM drive interface is?
   a. Parallel
   b. Serial
   c. IDE
   d. ESDI

23. External modems are usually connected to a
   a. Parallel port
   b. NIC
   c. Serial port
   d. MIDI port

24. Which statement is true about IRQs?

    a.   Devices share IRQs all the time

    b.   IRQs are stored in the Windows configuration files

    c.   After processing an IRQ, the CPU looks for others to process

    d.   Each device on a PC must have a unique IRQ

25. What does DMA stand for?

    a.   Direct memory access

    b.   Direct memory availability

    c.   Dual memory availability

    d.   Dual memory access

Chapter 3

Computer Assembly

Introduction

This chapter addresses the process of the computer assembly process. The ability to successfully assemble a computer is a milestone for the PC Ttechnician. It builds confidence and helps to demystify computer components. Although the process of assembling a computer is not dangerous, safety procedures must be followed in order to avoid hazardous situations. Review the safety precautions in Appendix C. Also, make sure the following important items are taken into account during the assembly process:

- Keep the work area free of clutter and clean.

- Food and drinks are not allowed in the work area.

- Remove all jewelry and watches.

- Make sure the power is off and the power plug has been removed when working inside the computer,

- Never look into a laser beam. Lasers are found in computer-related equipment.

- Make sure that the fire extinguisher and first aid kit is available.

- Cover sharp edges with tape when working inside the computer case.

- Monitors are out of the scope of this course. They can store up to 25,000 voltsDo not open or work on the monitor.

ESD Precautions

Electrostatic discharge (ESD) is more commonly referred to as static electricity. Static charges can build up in the body just by walking across the room. It might not be apparent, but it is usually enough to damage computer components if they are touched. A static charge of 2000 volts is enough for a person to notice – this may have been experienced when walking across a room and touching a doorknob or other metal surface. A static charge of only 200 volts is sufficient to damage a computer component. Be aware that damage can be done to a component through ESD without even realizing it.

ESD is probably the greatest enemy when unwrapping newly purchased computer parts and components and are ready to assemble the computer. List six precautions to take in the assembly process that will help prevent ESD related damage:

1. _____

2. _____

3. _____

4. _____

5. _____

6. _____

Creating a Computer Inventory

The first step in the computer assembly process is to get organized. A sample Inventory Checklist is provided in Appendix C. Besides the checklist, it is important to save all the documentation that comes with the components. Store original documentation in zip lock type bags and paper work in three-ring binders. Also, keep a notebook in which web sites can be referenced with useful information related to components such as devices drivers, and so on.

Describe a scenario where the inventory and related documentation would come in handy:

_____
_____
_____
_____
_____

Computer Components

There are two types of computer cases: desktop and tower. Tower cases include mini, mid-size, and full-size. List the factors that should be considered when determining the type of computer case to use:

_____
_____
_____
_____
_____

The power supply unit provides electrical power for every component inside the system unit. In the past, it also supplied alternating current (AC) to the display monitor. The computer power supply plays the critical role of converting commercial electrical power received from a 120-volts AC, 60-Hz (or 220-volts AC, 50-Hz outside the U.S.) outlet into other levels required by the components of the computer. The power supply unit also provides the system's ground.

There are two basic types of power supplies. List them:

1. _____

2. _____

A motherboard location map shows where the major components and hardware is located on the motherboard. A motherboard map can be found in the documentation that comes with the motherboard.

Why is it important to study the motherboard location map before proceeding with the installation?

_____

_____

_____

_____

_____

Configuring the motherboard is one of the most important tasks to accomplish when preparing the motherboard for installation of the various components.

The motherboard must be configured for the frequency of the _____
_____.

Hardware settings are made through the use of mini jumper connectors on the motherboard. Jumpers are devices that bridge pins on circuit boards. Closing or opening the circuits establishes logic levels to select functions for the operation of the board. (Data generally does not travel through these circuits.) On current technology motherboards, most of the jumpers relate to the central processing unit (CPU).

How are jumpers set and where is the information used to set the jumpers found?

_____

_____

_____

Several other jumper settings might have to be set along with the general motherboard configurations. Describe what each one is used for:

Basic Input/Output System (BIOS) recovery

_____

_____

Clear Complementary Metal Oxide Semiconductor (CMOS)

_____

_____

Password clear

_____

_____

BIOS setup access

_____

_____

Processor voltage

_____

_____

Configuring the motherboard typically means the following:

- Installing the CPU.

List the two main types of CPU interfaces:

_____ and _____

What happens if the proper voltage is not set? _____

_____

- Installing the heat sink and fan. What is a "boxed processor"?

_____

_____

- Installing RAM. Two common types of memory modules are used on most PCs. List them and explain the difference.

_____

_____

_____

Why should exact combinations be used when installing memory?_____

_____

_____

- Connecting the power supply cables to the motherboard power connectors and connecting miscellaneous connectors to the correct switches and status lights on the front case panel is completed after the motherboard has been installed in the computer case. Most modern connections are keyed. What does this mean?

_____

_____

Describe the steps to follow when installing a floppy drive.

1. _____

2. _____

3. _____

4. _____

5. _____

The steps to install a hard drive and CD-ROM drive are similar. Prior to installing these drives, the jumper settings must be set. The designation of a hard drive or CD-ROM drive as either master or slave is generally determined by the jumper configuration, not by the order in which the drive is daisy-chained to the other drive. What is the only exception?

_____

_____

_____

_____

_____

Briefly summarize the differences between the floppy drive and hard drive ribbon cables:

_____

_____

_____

The video card is the only expansion card that must be installed before booting the PC for the first time. Why?

_____

_____

_____

Final Steps

Use the Assembly Checklist in Appendix C to ensure that all items have been completed before closing the computer case. The final steps include connecting the keyboard, mouse, and the monitor. Plug the AC power cord into the back of the power supply and into the wall socket. The computer can now be turned on.

Booting the System for the First Time

What does BIOS stand for?

_____

What is the function of BIOS?

_____

Where is the BIOS and the information required to configure it stored?

_____

What does POST stand for and what does it do?

_____

_____

_____

It is especially important to get the BIOS set up right the first time the PC is booted up. Because the BIOS scans the system at boot time and compares what it finds against settings in CMOS, it must be properly configured to avoid errors.

Explain how to enter the BIOS setup.

_____

_____

_____

List the fields that are available for editing on the Standard CMOS setup screen:

1. _____

2. _____

3. _____

4. _____

5. _____

Discuss an advanced feature that can be set up in the BIOS Features setup screen.

_____

_____

_____

The Chipset Features setup screen allows the fine-tuning of the control parameters for the main system chipset. This chipset controls the following:

1. _____

2. _____

3. _____

4. _____

The Power Management setup screen controls the computer's optional power management for devices. When enabled, devices can be controlled to go into sleep or suspend mode. Why is it recommended that these features be disabled?

_____

_____

The Plug and Play/Peripheral Component Interconnect (PnP/PCI) Configuration screen contains the feature settings that control the system Input/Output (I/O) bus, IRQ, and direct memory access (DMA) allocation for Integrated Services Adapter (ISA) and PCI

Plug and Play devices. Of particular importance is the Resource Controlled By setting. Explain what this is used for.

_____

_____

_____

The Integrated Peripherals Configuration screen of the BIOS setup configures the control of peripherals such as the onboard floppy and hard drive controllers, USB controller, serial ports, parallel, and the sound card. Why would these features be set to Auto?

_____

_____

_____

When is Fixed Disk Detection used?

_____

_____

_____

What are the two password screens encountered in the BIOS setup, and explain when each would be important.

_____

_____

_____

_____

Explain POST errors and beep codes. Also, explain how to research beep codes.

_____

_____

_____

_____

_____

_____

_____

_____

_____

_____

_____

_____

_____

_____

Concept Question

The computer is assembled and it works! What was learned from the process that will be useful the next time you build a computer?

_____
_____
_____
_____
_____
_____
_____
_____
_____
_____
_____
_____
_____
_____
_____

Additional Notes

_____
_____
_____
_____
_____
_____
_____
_____
_____
_____
_____
_____
_____
_____

Labs and Worksheets

The following labs and worksheets are available in *CISCO NETWORKING ACADEMY PROGRAM IT Essentials I: PC Hardware and Software Lab Companion* and as part of the online curriculum. Labs and worksheets are an excellent tool that you can use to help reinforce the material covered in this chapter.

Labs:

3.3.4	The Computer Case and Power Supply
3.5.3	Motherboard Installation
3.6.4	Floppy Drive, Hard Drive, and CD-ROM Installation
3.7.1	Video Card Installation and System Booting

Worksheets:

3.3.4	Power Supplies
3.9.1	What is BIOS?

A+ Exam Review Questions

The following are review questions for the A+ exam. Answers are found in Appendix A.

1. What does ESD stand for?
    a.   Electronic stasis device

    b.   Electrostatic discharge

    c.   Electric surge device

    d.   Electronic system driver

2. How do you best prevent damaging a computer with static electricity?
    a.   Always use a rubber mat as a work surface

    b.   Always touch a ground point on the chassis to discharge static

    c.   Always take off your shoes before working inside a computer

    d.   Always wear an ESD strap when working inside a computer

3. To help prevent ESD, humidity levels should be kept at?
    a.   Between 20 percent and 30 percent

    b.   Exactly 50 percent

    c.   Humidity is not a factor

    d.   Above 50 percent

4. The PC power supply
    a.   Provides AC current to the system components

    b.   Converts AC power to DC power

    c.   Connects the computers components to a power source

    d.   Protects the computer components against power surges

5. The power supply voltage can be checked by measuring the P8 and P9 connections with a?
    a.   Multiprobe

    b.   Cable tester

    c.   Multimeter

    d.   Battery

6. What is a memory bank?

    a. The cache where memory is stored

    b. The actual slot that memory goes into

    c. The collection of all memory

    d. Virtual memory

7. The correct positioning when installing SIMM modules is indicated by a?

    a. Missing pin

    b. Red stripe

    c. Notch on one end

    d. Red 1

8. To install a DIMM module, you need to?

    a. Line up straight over the socket and press in

    b. Tilt 45 degrees and push

    c. Press down on the lever

    d. Line up all metal pins and slide

9. Which components reside in expansion slots on the motherboard?

    a. CPU, RAM, and power plugs

    b. Keyboard, mouse, and printer

    c. Network interface, sound, and SCSI cards

    d. CD-ROM, floppy, and hard drives

10. The purpose of expansion slots is to?

    a. Expand the CPU

    b. Allow the hard drive and floppy drive to communicate with the CPU

    c. Add processing power to the computer

    d. Allow the addition of optional components

11. Care should be taken when handling an expansion card. Do not touch the?

    a. Metal bracket

    b. Metal edge connectors

    c. Corners of the card

    d. Connector slots

12. Which type of expansion card is configured using software instead of jumpers?
    a.   Configured cards
    b.   32-bit cards
    c.   16-bit cards
    d.   Plug and Play cards

13. When you connect a ribbon cable, install the connector by?
    a.   Connecting the black stripe to pin #1
    b.   Connecting the black stripe to pin #2
    c.   Connecting the red stripe to pin #1
    d.   Connecting the red stripe to pin #2

14. When installing an IDE drive, which jumper settings are not a factor?
    a.   Single
    b.   Slave
    c.   Master
    d.   Secondary

15. The length of cable for an IDE/ATA hard drive is limited to?
    a.   It is not limited
    b.   12" exactly
    c.   18" and less
    d.   20" or more

16. How should the jumpers be set on your IDE CD-ROM drive when it is attached to the primary IDE adapter with your hard drive?
    a.   Master
    b.   Slave
    c.   Remove the jumpers
    d.   Auto

17. Plugging in or unplugging a keyboard with the power turned on can damage the?
    a.   Hard drive
    b.   Mouse
    c.   Motherboard
    d.   Keyboard

18. A mouse plugs into a?
   a.   RJ11 port
   b.   PS/2 or USB
   c.   Parallel port
   d.   RJ45 port

19. How are PCI devices configured?
   a.   During DOS boot
   b.   The Internet
   c.   Windows setup
   d.   They are always self-configuring

20. How many pins are there in an IDE connector?
   a.   80
   b.   50
   c.   68
   d.   40

21. The length of a SCSI cable is determined by the?
   a.   Number of devices
   b.   Computer's speed
   c.   SCSI device
   d.   Thickness of the cable

22. A technique that loads the system BIOS from ROM into system RAM during the boot is?
   a.   Fault tolerance
   b.   Int19
   c.   Shadowing
   d.   Loading

23. Basic instructions for CPU and I/O device communication are located in?
   a.   CMOS
   b.   Windows configuration files
   c.   DOS
   d.   BIOS

24. Which software or firmware routine is executed first during the computer boot up procedure?
    a. BIOS
    b. CMOS
    c. CONFIG.SYS
    d. WIN.INI

25. Circuit boards or devices should not be added or removed?
    a. Until software is installed
    b. With a grounding strap on
    c. Until the computer is not busy
    d. With power on

Chapter 4

Operating System Fundamentals

Introduction

The focus of this chapter is the operating system (OS). This is the software that controls thousands of operations, provides an interface between the user and the computer, and runs applications. Basically, the OS is in charge of running the computer. Today, most computer systems are sold with an operating system already installed. Computers that are designed for individual users (called personal computers or PCs) have operating systems that are designed for individuals running small jobs. An OS is designed to control the operations of programs such as Web browsers, word processors, and e-mail programs.

With the development of processor technology, computers have become capable of executing more and more instructions per second. These advances have made it possible to run operating systems that are capable of running many complex tasks simultaneously. When a computer needs to accommodate concurrent users and multiple jobs, Information Technology (IT) professionals usually turn to faster computers that have more robust operating systems.

Computers that are capable of handling concurrent users and multiple jobs are often called network servers or simply servers. Servers have operating systems installed called Network Operating Systems (NOSs). A fast computer with a NOS installed can run a large company or Internet site, which involves keeping track of many users and programs.

Three basic elements make up the major design components of any operating system.

1. _____ is the part of the OS that issues commands by either typing them at a command prompt or by pointing and clicking the mouse.

2. _____ is the core of the OS. It is responsible for loading and running programs and managing input and output.

3. The _____ is what the OS uses to organize and manage files.

What does the term modular mean in relation to the components of an OS?

_____
_____
_____
_____

Operating System Functions

All operating systems perform the same basic functions regardless of the size or complexity of the computer or its operating system. Provide a brief description for each of the following functions:

File and folder management:

_____
_____
_____
_____

Management of applications:

_____
_____
_____
_____

Support for built-in utility programs:

_____
_____
_____
_____

Access control to computer's hardware:

_____
_____
_____
_____

Will a program written for a Windows-based OS work on UNIX? Why or why not?

_____
_____
_____
_____

List three of the most popular operating systems. Indicate which are proprietary and which are not:

1. _____
   _____

2. _____
_____

3. _____
_____

Operating System Vocabulary

To understand what an OS is capable of, it is important to understand some basic terms. The following terms are often used when comparing operating systems:

Multiuser: _____
_____
_____

Multitasking: _____
_____
_____

Multiprocessing: _____
_____
_____

Multithreading: _____
_____
_____

GUI: _____
_____
_____

Disk Operating System (DOS)

DOS was developed in 1981. It is a collection of programs and commands that control the overall computer operation in a disk-based system. DOS is responsible for finding and organizing data and applications on the disk.

The basic elements of DOS include the following:

- DOS is a command line operating system; it is not user-friendly. The best way to learn DOS is to use it.

- DOS can only run one program at a time. It is not multitasking.

- DOS can only run small programs and has memory limitations.

- DOS is an essential tool for IT professionals and is used extensively for troubleshooting.

Three distinct sections make up DOS. List them:

1. _____
   _____

2. _____
   _____

3. _____
   _____

In DOS, the user interface is the _____
_____

DOS Commands

The introduction of operating systems having a GUI, such as Microsoft Windows, has made DOS mostly obsolete. DOS however, continues to play a significant role in programming and for technical purposes. All generations of Windows support DOS, which makes it an extremely important tool for the PC technician. Provide the function for each DOS command listed, and indicate if it is an internal or external function.

Command	Internal/External	Function
DIR		
CD		
MD		
RD		
DEL		
REN		
SET		
MEM		
COPY		
TYPE		

FDISK		
TIME		
DATE		
CHKDSK		
DISKCOPY		
EDIT		
FORMAT		
PRINT		
ATTRIB		
.		

Many of the DOS commands can be modified by placing one or more software switches at the end of the basic command. Switches are options that can be added to a command that will modify the output of the command. A switch is added to the command by adding a **space**, a forward-slash (/), and a single letter. The format is as follows:

COMMAND **(space)** */switch*

For example, **C:\>DIR /w**

In the example given above, the **/w** is a switch. The **/w** modifies the **dir** command by presenting the screen output information in a wide format that is across the screen.

List the common switches used with the **Attrib** command and the function of each:

_____   _____

_____   _____

What is the function of the + and - sign? _____

_____

List the common switch used with the **Del** command and its function:

_____   _____

List the common switches used with the **Edit** command and the function of each:

_____   _____

_____   _____

List the common switches used with the **Format** command and the function of each:

_____   _____

List the common switch used with the **FDISK** command and the function of each:

_____   _____

List the common switches used with the **Scandisk** command and the function of each:

_____   _____
_____   _____

List the common switches used with the **mem** command and the function of each:

_____   _____
_____   _____

List the common switches used with the **copy** command and the function of each:

_____   _____
_____   _____
_____   _____

The following commands do not use switches:

_____   _____
_____   _____

What does the **more** command display? _____

_____

To understand basic DOS commands, first look at the structure of the disk. The way that programs and data are stored on a disk is set up much like a filing cabinet. In DOS, they are called files and are grouped together in directories. Directories are much like the folders in the file cabinet. This process organizes the files and directories for easier retrieval and use. It is time consuming to find a single form in a file cabinet if the form is not held in a specific place. Directories can be nested inside other directories, just like a folder placed inside another folder. Nested directories are referred to as subdirectories. Directories became known as folders in the Windows OS.

List the common attributes for DOS files:

1. _____

_____

2. _____

_____

3. _____
   _____

4. _____
   _____

Hard drives organize the disk into directories and subdirectories. The main directory is known as the _____
_____.

All other directories, if they exist, radiate (branch out), similar to the branches of a tree. In MS-DOS, a graphical representation of the disk drive's directory organization is called a _____.

A **DOS boot disk** boots a computer to the DOS prompt. List the three files that the boot disk must contain.

1. _____
   _____

2. _____
   _____

3. _____
   _____

How do you create a DOS boot disk?

_____
_____
_____
_____
_____

What is the difference between a boot disk and a bootable disk?

_____
_____
_____
_____
_____

Memory Management

The operating system that runs the computer uses two main types of memory:

- System memory (random-access memory [RAM]), also known as physical memory

- Virtual memory

Four categories of system memory are in the operating system. Provide a brief explanation of each:

Conventional memory: _____
_____
_____
_____

Upper memory/Expanded memory: _____
_____
_____
_____

Extended memory: _____
_____
_____
_____

High memory: _____
_____
_____
_____

Memory Management Tools

Several tools can be used to manage and optimize system memory. Below are a few memory management tools available. Explain how each of the following tools helps to adjust and optimize the system memory:

EMM386.EXE: _____
_____
_____
_____

HIMEM.SYS: _____
_____
_____
_____
_____

DOS=HIGH: _____
_____
_____
_____
_____

DEVICEHIGH/LOADHIGH: _____
_____
_____
_____
_____

Concept Question

The concepts of real versus. protected mode memory addressing come up frequently in discussions of memory space located above conventional memory; that is, all memory above 1024 KB. Explain the difference between Real Mode and Protected Mode:

_____
_____
_____
_____
_____
_____
_____
_____
_____
_____
_____
_____
_____
_____

Additional Notes

_____
_____
_____
_____
_____
_____
_____
_____
_____
_____
_____
_____
_____
_____
_____
_____
_____
_____
_____

Labs and Worksheets

The following labs and worksheets are available in CISCO NETWORKING ACADEMY PROGRAM IT Essentials I: PC Hardware and Software Lab Companion and as part of the online curriculum. Labs and worksheets are an excellent tool that you can use to help reinforce the material covered in this chapter.

Labs:

4.2.3   Basic DOS Commands (PDF, 34 KB)
4.2.4   Creating a DOS Boot Disk (PDF, 10 KB)

Worksheets:

4.1.3   Operating System Fundamentals (PDF, 6 KB)
4.2.3   DOS Commands (PDF, 6 KB)
4.2.7   DOS (PDF, 6 KB)

A+ Exam Review Questions

The following are review questions for the A+ exam. Answers are found in Appendix A.

1. What is the definition of an operating system?
   a. Software that executes other software
   b. An interface between a user and software
   c. Software that controls thousands of operations and provides an interface between the user and the computer
   d. Software manipulated by hardware

2. Which of the following is not a valid OS?
   a. DOS
   b. Windows
   c. LAN
   d. UNIX

3. What does DOS stand for?
   a. Disk Operating Sectors
   b. Disk Operating System
   c. Disk Operating Services
   d. Disk Organizing Software

4. What is the maximum length of a DOS filename?
   a. Up to 8 characters with an extension of 3 characters
   b. Up to 12 characters, the extension is optional
   c. 16 characters with an extension of 4 characters
   d. 32 characters with an extension of 3 characters

5. What are the three DOS files that can start the operating system?
   a. AUTOEXEC.BAT, IO.SYS, COMMAND.COM
   b. IO.SYS, COMMAND.COM, SYSTEM.INI
   c. IO.SYS, MSDOS.SYS, COMMAND.COM
   d. WIN.INI, SYSTEM.INI, COMMAND.COM

6. Where is the statement LOADHI or LH used?
   a. CONFIG.SYS
   b. AUTOEXEC.BAT
   c. SYSTEM.INI
   d. MSDOS.SYS

7. When typing in DOS, which program is a good shortcut tool?
   a. Msd
   b. Dir
   c. Cls
   d. Doskey

8. What does the DOS command VER show?
   a. The current system variables
   b. The current version of the OS
   c. The current version of BIOS
   d. The current version of the Registry

9. Which of the following is an external DOS command?
   a. DIR
   b. Help
   c. Copy
   d. CLS

10. Which of the following is an internal DOS command?
    a. Graphics
    b. Unerase
    c. Diskcopy
    d. DIR

11. How do you show all the system files within a directory?
    a. DIR*.SYS
    b. DIR SYS
    c. DIR SYS /ALL
    d. DIR*.SYS/ALL

12. The .ini file type usually contains what type of information?

    a.   Where files used by the operating system reside

    b.   The names and locations of startup files

    c.   User instructions

    d.   Parameter information about a program

13. What does the DEVICE= statement in CONFIG.SYS mean?

    a.   It identifies the devices on the computer

    b.   It sets up the driver configuration

    c.   It tells the OS what drivers are running

    d.   It loads a device driver

14. What is the memory address from 640 KB – 1024KB called?

    a.   Common memory

    b.   Upper memory area

    c.   Basic memory

    d.   Conventional memory

15. What is the memory address from 0 to 640 KB called?

    a.   Common memory

    b.   Basic memory

    c.   Usable memory

    d.   Conventional memory

16. What is extended memory?

    a.   All memory above 640 KB

    b.   Memory between 640 KB and 1024 KB

    c.   All memory after 640 KB

    d.   All memory after 1024 KB

17. What is the first 64 KB of extended memory called?

    a.   XMS: Extended memory specification

    b.   UMB: Upper memory block

    c.   HMA: High memory area

    d.   Conventional memory

18. What is virtual memory?
   a. Swapping memory in and out of the high memory area
   b. Simulating more memory by swapping files between RAM and the hard drive
   c. Paging memory between conventional memory and the HMA
   d. Using the extended memory area to simulate expanded memory

19. If the HIMEM.SYS file is corrupt or missing, what will happen?
   a. Windows will start in safe mode
   b. Windows will load but applications will not run
   c. Windows 98 will load but will not use more than 640 KB
   d. Windows 98 will not load

20. What program is used to find and repair lost clusters?
   a. Scandisk
   b. Defrag
   c. MSD
   d. DOS

21. Which program sets up a partition on a hard drive?
   a. Partition
   b. Fdisk
   c. Format
   d. Diskpart

22. What file should not be edited by the user?
   a. CONFIG.SYS
   b. WIN.INI
   c. AUTOEXEC.BAT
   d. HIMEM.SYS

23. The three system files needed by the system to boot to DOS are?
   a. IO.SYS, MSDOS.SYS, COMMAND.COM
   b. IO.SYS, AUTOEXEC.BAT, MSDOS.SYS
   c. COMMAND.COM, CONFIG.SYS, MSDOS.SYS
   d. IO.SYS, AUTOEXEC.BAT, COMMAND.COM

24.   Why would a read-only attribute be applied to a file?

   a.   So it cannot be changed

   b.   So it can only be read by DOS

   c.   So changes can be tracked

   d.   So the user knows it is a system file

25.   How do you step through the startup files when DOS starts?

   a.   F5

   b.   F6

   c.   Shift + F8

   d.   Shift + F5

Chapter 5

Windows 9x Operating Systems

Introduction

Windows 9x refers to Windows 95, OSR2, Windows 98, and Windows Millennium. As one of the most popular operating systems today, it is designed to run on PCs using an Intel-compatible CPU. Windows-based PCs use a graphical user interface (GUI) as the interface between the computer and the user. The Windows operating system is designed to be run and maintained by a single user.

The focus of this chapter is on installing Windows 98 and understanding the basics of this operating system. This includes navigating the Desktop, the file structure, and the file management system. The first step in the installation of Windows 98 is preparing the hard drive.

Preparing a Hard Drive

When a new hard drive is installed it is completely blank. To install an operating system, the hard drive must be set up.

What program creates partitions, the boot sector, and the partition table?

_____

Provide a brief definition for the following:

Primary partition:

_____
_____
_____

Extended partition:

_____
_____
_____

Active partition:

_____

_____

_____

Logical drive:

_____

_____

_____

Boot sector:

_____

_____

_____

Partition table:

_____

_____

_____

Formatting:

_____

_____

_____

Cluster:

_____

_____

_____

FAT:

_____

_____

_____

Installing Windows 98

The following are the requirements for Installing Windows 98:

- An 80486DX/66MHz or faster processor, operating with at least 16 MB of random-access memory (RAM). A recommended minimum of 32 MB of RAM; or ideally, 64 MB of RAM if the system can support it.
- The system must possess a keyboard, a mouse, and a 16-color VGA monitor or better (SVGA recommended).
- The system's hard drive needs to have between 255 and 355 MB of free space available to successfully install the full version of Windows 98 on a FAT16 drive or 175 and 255 MB of drive space on a FAT32 drive.
- To upgrade from Windows 95 requires about 195 MB of free hard disk space, but can range from between 120 MB and 255 MB, depending on the options that are installed.
- Sometimes a modem is required to download device driver upgrades from various sources on the Internet. The minimum required is a 14.4 kbps (28.8 kbps or faster is recommended).
- 3.5-inch high density floppy disk drive and CD-ROM drive (32 speed is recommended).

Most of the steps in the installation are automated through a built-in utility called Setup. An understanding of each stage of the installation or setup process will be useful when performing an actual installation or for troubleshooting. The steps of the installation procedure are divided into four phases.

Provide a brief explanation of each of the phases:

1. Preparing to run Windows 98 Setup

   _____
   _____
   _____
   _____
   _____
   _____

2. Collecting information about your computer

   _____
   _____
   _____
   _____
   _____
   _____

3. Copying Windows 98 files and restarting the computer

_____
_____
_____
_____
_____
_____

4. Setting up hardware and finalizing settings

_____
_____
_____
_____
_____
_____

What are the advantages of installing Windows from the hard drive?

_____
_____
_____
_____
_____
_____

To install Windows 98 onto a new, or a reformatted disk drive, it is necessary to boot the system from the Windows distribution CD or to run the SETUP.EXE program from the DOS prompt. Using this method, the Windows 98 Setup program runs a real-mode version (looking at all files) of the Scandisk utility on the drive.

What does Scandisk do?

_____
_____
_____
_____
_____

Troubleshooting

Knowing the various tips and tricks in troubleshooting a Windows installation can make the difference between a technician and an excellent technician.

In general, when troubleshooting any microprocessor-based equipment such as the PC, it is good practice to begin from the outside of the system and move inwards. Proceed in a systematic way as follows:

1. Start the system in a logical order to see what symptoms are produced.

2. Isolate the problem as either software- or hardware-related.

3. Determine the nature of the problem and isolate it to a particular section of the hardware or software.

4. Determine the appropriate solution.

Most successful troubleshooting results from careful observation combined with deductive reasoning and an organized approach to solving problems.

Error Resolution

You've installed Windows 98 and restarted the computer. Unfortunately, the first boot process is hanging for no apparent reason. Describe the steps that you would take and the specific items you would check to correct this problem:

_____
_____
_____
_____
_____
_____
_____
_____
_____
_____
_____
_____
_____

Windows 98 Help Tools

Help tools refers to troubleshooting software that is either built-in to Windows or available from a third party. These tools are used during the installation should any problem occur and for preventive maintenance.

Provide a brief description for each of the following:

Safe Mode/Device Manager

_____
_____
_____
_____
_____
_____
_____

Scandisk/Defrag

_____
_____
_____
_____
_____
_____
_____

Virus Scan

_____
_____
_____
_____
_____
_____
_____

Fdsik/MBR

_____
_____
_____
_____
_____
_____
_____

Setup Errors

Setup errors can be challenging for the PC technician. Describe the best course of action for the following errors:

Not enough disk space:

_____
_____
_____
_____
_____
_____

Not enough memory:

_____
_____
_____
_____
_____
_____

Setup has detected that an earlier version of SetupX.dll or Neti.dll is in use:

_____
_____
_____
_____
_____
_____

CAB file error message:

_____
_____
_____
_____
_____

Unrecoverable setup error. Setup cannot continue on this system configuration:

_____

_____

_____

_____

_____

_____

Setup cannot create files on the startup drive and cannot set up Windows 98. There may be too many files in the root directory of the startup drive or the startup drive letter may have been remapped (SU0018):

_____

_____

_____

_____

_____

_____

Setup cannot write to the temporary directory:

_____

_____

_____

_____

_____

_____

SU0011:

_____

_____

_____

_____

_____

System Properties

The computer's System Properties has four categories of information. Click the tab to access the information. The four categories are as follows:

1. _____

2. _____

3. _____

4. _____

The Device Manager is included with Windows 98, and allows the user to manage, view, and change computer resources. The Device Manager in Windows provides a graphical interface representation of the devices configured in the system.

What does an exclamation point inside a yellow circle indicate?

_____
_____
_____

What does a red X at a device icon indicate?

_____
_____
_____

Other Devices displays in place of an icon. What does that indicate?

_____
_____
_____

Device drivers give today's PCs the ability to add a wide variety of devices to the system. A device driver is software that is specially designed to enable the computer to see the hardware or devices installed within the system and enables the device to function properly. List the two ways to install a device driver:

1. _____
_____

2. _____
_____

A Windows 98 startup disk is essential if the system crashes, hangs up on startup, or when Windows 98 setup fails before completion. Windows 98 setup is easier with a Windows 98 startup disk.

Describe a situation where a startup disk would be used:

_____
_____
_____

Sometimes it is necessary to remove the Windows OS that is installed on a system. The uninstall procedure allows the system to return to a previous version of the Windows OS.

In some instances, uninstalling Windows 98 is the only solution left when an attempted upgrade fails, especially if no system backup was done before trying to upgrade.

When can Windows 98 be uninstalled?

_____

_____

_____

When can Windows 98 NOT be uninstalled?

_____

_____

_____

Windows Features and Functions

Windows 98 is a major upgrade to Windows 95. It provides performance enhancements and support for more hardware, including the Universal Serial Bus (USB). It supports two monitors, which, for example, allows developers to work on one resolution and test on another. Windows 98 also integrates Microsoft's Internet Explorer Web browser into the Desktop.

Demonstrate knowledge of the Windows 98 features and functions by answering the following:

List the two ways most commonly used to access files and programs:

1. _____

2. _____

The Windows file structure in Explorer displays the hierarchical structure of files, folders, and drives on a computer. The comparison is to a tree.

The trunk relates to the: _____

Major branches relate to the: _____

Minor branches relate to the: _____

Leaves relate to the: _____

There are two ways to create a new folder in Explorer. Explain one way to add a subfolder to the My Documents folder.

_____

_____

_____

_____

_____

Windows 3.1 and DOS file names are limited to eight letters plus a three-letter suffix, which is called an extension (this DOS format is referred to as 8+3).

Windows 98 and later allows extended filenames. How many characters can a Windows 98 file or folder have? _____

What is the significance of the extension of the filename?

_____

_____

_____

_____

What are illegal characters in a Windows 98 filename? List them:_____

_____

_____

_____

_____

What is the Recycle Bin used for?

_____

_____

_____

_____

What is the easiest way to print a document?

_____

_____

_____

_____

Describe the steps required to add a new network printer to a PC.

_____
_____
_____
_____
_____
_____
_____
_____

A program on a PC is no longer needed and must be deleted to free up space on the hard drive. Describe the appropriate way to do this.

_____
_____
_____
_____

Concept Question

The importance of backing up the computer system cannot be stressed enough. As the head of the technical department of a large corporation, describe your policy on keeping the system and files safe.

_____
_____
_____
_____
_____
_____
_____
_____
_____
_____
_____
_____
_____
_____
_____
_____
_____

Additional Notes

_____
_____
_____
_____
_____
_____
_____
_____
_____
_____
_____
_____
_____
_____

Labs and Worksheets

The following labs and worksheets are available in *CISCO NETWORKING ACADEMY PROGRAM IT Essentials I: PC Hardware and Software Lab Companion* and as part of the online curriculum. Labs and worksheets are an excellent tool that you can use to help reinforce the material covered in this chapter.

Labs:

5.1.6	Change File Views in Windows (showing file extensions)
5.1.7	Text Editing and File Management
5.4.2	Hard Drive Preparation Using FDISK and FORMAT
5.5.5	Windows OS Installation
5.6.1	Troubleshooting 101
5.6.4	Installing a Driver
5.6.5	Windows Startup Disk

Worksheets:

5.1.10	Windows Files and Folders
5.2.2	Managing Printers
5.4.2	Hard Drive Preparation
5.6.6	Troubleshooting the Windows Installation

A+ Exam Review Questions

The following are review questions for the A+ exam. Answers are found in Appendix A.

1.   What does the operating system do?
    a.   Boots the computer
    b.   Operates the hardware
    c.   Translates human language to computer language
    d.   Allows users to operate equipment connected to a computer

2.   What is the first thing that needs to be done with a new hard drive?
    a.   FDISK
    b.   Format
    c.   Scandisk
    d.   Defrag

3.   What is the second thing that needs to be done with a new hard drive?
    a.   FDISK
    b.   Format
    c.   Scandisk
    d.   Degrag

4.   In Windows 98, what utilities set up the hard drive?
    a.   Scandisk and Newdrive
    b.   Scandisk and FDISK
    c.   FDISK and Format
    d.   Scandisk and Format

5.   What is another name for the active partition?
    a.   Bootable partition
    b.   Usable partition
    c.   First partition
    d.   Logical partition

6. How many logical drives can be created by FDISK on an EIDE drive?
    a. 4
    b. 8
    c. 16
    d. 24

7. What locates the OS during the boot up process?
    a. Boot sector
    b. System.ini
    c. Boot cylinder
    d. Boot track

8. When installing Window 98, what is the lowest DOS version that will allow it?
    a. Version 3.2
    b. Version 3
    c. An existing OS is only required when using the upgrade version
    d. It is not necessary to have an operating system installed

9. How do you find out why Windows 98 crashes or hangs during the hardware detection phase of the installation?
    a. Examine the crash.log file
    b. Examine the crashdet.log file
    c. Examine the crash.txt file
    d. Examine the crashdet.txt file

10. Is it possible to upgrade a Windows 98 computer to Window NT?
    a. Yes
    b. No
    c. Only if you have 64 MB of memory
    d. Only if you have 32 MB of memory

11. What does Scandisk do?
    a. Removes viruses from the hard drive
    b. Erases temporary files from the hard drive
    c. Erases bad clusters
    d. Marks bad clusters

12. What program edits the registry?

    a.   Edit

    b.   Registry

    c.   Sysedit

    d.   Regedit

13. What should you do if the Windows 98 installation procedure fails?

    a.   Remove any hardware listed in the error.txt file

    b.   Restart the computer using Safe Mode

    c.   Remove any hardware listed in the fault.txt file

    d.   Use a clean boot disk to start the computer

14. What does the IO.SYS file do in Windows 98?

    a.   Loads the basic device drivers and sets the basic system headings

    b.   Tells the OS which hardware the user has access to

    c.   Controls the video system of the computer

    d.   Tells the OS which software the user has access to

15. Where in Windows 98 can you remove or view devices and their properties?

    a.   **Control panel > Devices**

    b.   Device Manager

    c.   **System > Devices**

    d.   **Start > Devices**

16. In Windows 98, how do you make an emergency disk?

    a.   **Start > Programs > Startup > Bootdisk**

    b.   **Control Panel > Add/Remove Programs > Startup disk tab > Create Disk**

    c.   **Start > Programs > Add/Remove Programs > Startup Disk Tab > Create Disk**

    d.   Double-click **My Computer**, go to **Add/Remove Programs > Startup Disk Tab > Create Disk**

17. How do you restore a file if you delete it from the Windows 98 desktop?

    a.   **Start > Control Panel > Undelete**

    b.   **Start > Programs > Undelete**

    c.   **Recycle Bin > Restore**

    d.   My Computer

18. By default, how much space on the hard drive is set aside for the Recycle Bin in Windows 98?

   a. 10 percent

   b. 20 percent

   c. 30 percent

   d. 40 percent

19. How can you view the version of Windows that is currently installed?

   a. **Start > Help > About**

   b. Right-click My Computer and Properties

   c. Right-click My Computer and Version

   d. **Start > Help > Version**

20. How do you view the file or folder properties in Windows 98?

   a. Left-click the icon and select Properties

   b. Right-click the icon and select Properties

   c. Drop the icon on the Taskbar

   d. **Start > Properties**, and enter the name of the object

21. How do you locate an object in Windows 98?

   a. **Start > Settings > Find**

   b. My Computer, go to **Settings > Find**

   c. **Start > Help > Find**

   d. **Start > Find**

22. What character CANNOT be used when naming a DOS file?

   a. ~ (tilde)

   b. > (greater than sign)

   c. – (dash)

   d. _ (underscore)

23. If a printer is changed in DOS, what must be done?

   a. Change the DOS printer driver

   b. Change each application printer driver

   c. Change the printer in CMOS

   d. DOS will find the printer driver automatically

24. What does creating a shortcut in Windows 98 allow the user to do?
    a. Find shortcuts more easily
    b. Execute applications more easily
    c. Have quick access to executables
    d. Make usc of the Desktop

25. Windows 98 does not support which types of applications?
    a. DOS programs
    b. UNIX programs
    c. 16-bit Windows programs
    d. 32-bit Windows programs

Chapter 6

PC Multimedia

Introduction

This chapter discusses the multimedia capabilities of the PC. Included is an overview of the components required to produce multimedia on the PC and how they work.

The technology to create and display multimedia is evolving at an incredible rate. The term multimedia typically means the combination of text, sound, or motion video. Although generally described as the addition of animated images (for example an animated GIF on the web), multimedia actually includes the addition of the following:

- Text and sound

- Text, sound, and still or animated graphic images

- Text, sound, and video images

- Video and sound

- Multiple display areas, images, or presentations presented concurrently

- In live situations, the use of a speaker or actors and props together with sound, images, and motion video

Multimedia is distinguished from traditional motion pictures or movies both by the scale of the production (multimedia is usually smaller and less expensive) and by the addition of audience participation or interactive multimedia. Interactive elements can include voice command, mouse manipulation, text entry, touch screen, video capture of the user, or live participation (as in live presentations).

PC Requirements to Run Multimedia

The types of computer hardware and software necessary to develop multimedia on the PC vary. The minimum hardware requirements include a computer monitor, video accelerator card, and a sound adapter card with attached speakers. Additionally, the following components provide visual and sound output.

- A microphone connected to a plug on the sound adapter card inputs sound.

- CDs and DVD players are common PC components used for input and output.

- A connection to the Internet through a network interface card (NIC) or a modem also provides multimedia input to the system. Streaming of audio and video is popular.

- Digital still pictures and video cameras are often connected through standard computer ports or special card adapters.

- A video capture card, which is a special adapter card that samples and converts the images and sounds, can provide television and radio recordings and images.

- MPEG hardware and Web-based movie players play movies.

- Computer games through a DVD or CD require specialized hardware.

A video adapter or video card is an integrated circuit card in the computer or in some cases the monitor that provides digital-to-analog conversion, video random-access memory (RAM), and a video controller so that date can be sent to a computer's display. Explain the following related terms:

VGA: _____
_____
_____
_____
_____
_____
_____
_____
_____

VESA: _____
_____
_____
_____
_____
_____
_____
_____

Display: _____
_____
_____
_____
_____
_____
_____
_____

CRT: _____
_____
_____
_____
_____
_____
_____
_____

LCD: _____
_____
_____
_____
_____
_____
_____
_____
_____

VDT: _____
_____
_____
_____
_____
_____
_____
_____
_____

VDU: _____
_____
_____
_____
_____
_____
_____
_____

VDT: _____
_____
_____
_____
_____
_____
_____
_____

VDU: _____
_____
_____
_____
_____
_____
_____
_____

Computer displays can be characterized by the following. Provide a definition for each:

1. Color capability: _____
    _____
    _____

2. Sharpness and viewability: _____
    _____
    _____

3. Size of the screen: _____
    _____
    _____

4. Projection technology: _____
    _____
    _____

To date, two common data-compression standards are used with digitized video. These are the Joint Photographic Experts Group (JPEG) and the Moving Picture Experts Group (MPEG) compression standards.

Another data-compression method used with PCs is the Indeo compression standard, developed by Intel. Indeo is similar to the MPEG standard, in that it was actually designed to be a distribution format. It was primarily intended to play back compressed video files from the smallest file size possible. Later versions of this standard include the MPEG compression methods.

Another compression/decompression standard supported by video for Windows is Cinepak. This standard uses an AVI file format to produce 40:1 compression ratios and 30-frames per second capture, at 320 x 200 resolution. Windows 95 naturally supports several different compression techniques. These include Cinepak, two versions of Indeo, an RLE format, and the Video 1 format

Why is compression important in multimedia?

_____
_____
_____
_____
_____
_____
_____
_____
_____

Upgrading Video

The Accelerated Graphics Port (AGP) interface is a variation of the Peripheral Component Interconnect (PCI) bus design that has been modified to handle the intense data throughput associated with three-dimensional graphics. What are the advantages of an AGP?

_____
_____
_____
_____
_____
_____

Video capture software captures frames of television video and converts them into digital formats that can be processed by the system. Graphics packages can manipulate the contents of the video after it has been converted into digital formats that the computer can handle. One of the popular file formats for video is the Microsoft Audio Visual Interface (AVI) format.

Video capture cards are responsible for converting video signals from different sources into digital signals that can be manipulated by the computer. As in the audio conversion process, the video card samples the incoming video signal by feeding it through an analog-to-digital (A-to-D) converter.

What is YUV format?

_____
_____
_____

Explain Color Space Conversion

_____
_____
_____

In addition to changing the format, the capture card also scales the image to fit in the defined video window on the monitor's screen. The capture card's video signal processor adjusts the image to the correct size by interpolating (adding or removing) adjacent pixels as necessary. The encoder samples the analog signal at a rate of 27 MB per second. This value becomes important when you realize that, at this rate, a 500 MB hard drive would be full in 18.5 seconds.

What does RAMDAC stand for and what does it do?_____

_____

_____

_____

_____

_____

_____

_____

_____

_____

_____

_____

_____

_____

Audio Capabilities

Audio is an integral component of the multimedia experience and is a standard feature on personal computers. Educational and recreational software uses sound effects to heighten the experience. Musicians use the computer's audio capabilities to create songs. Visually impaired users can have the computer read information to them.

The applications for computer audio are endless but for a PC to have audio capabilities, it requires the use of a sound card.

A sound card is a device (either in the form of an expansion card or a chipset) that allows the computer to handle audio information. A sound card has three basic functions – list them:

1. _____

2. _____

3. _____

Even though there are many types of sound cards available for different applications, every sound card has the following basic components:

- **Processor**—The digital signal processor (DSP) is a chip (or set of chips) that is the brain of the sound card. The DSP handles the basic instructions that drive the sound card as well as the routing of audio information. It can also act as the synthesizer, or music generator.

- **Converters**—Digital-to-analog (DAC) and analog-to-digital (ADC) converters are used in the input and output process. Most audio information recorded from outside of the computer (unless in a digital format) must pass through the ADC and data that is being output to speakers uses the services of the DAC.

- **Memory**—More advanced sound cards use memory to store samples from musical instruments and to hold instructions for Musical Instrument Digital Interface (MIDI) devices. This memory is usually in the form of read-only memory (ROM), Flash, or non-volatile RAM (NVRAM) and can often be upgraded or expanded.

- **Ports**—Sound cards can have multiple internal and external ports for connecting to input and output devices. Also known as jacks or interfaces, these ports expand the functionality of a sound card

Sound cards produce audio (synthesize) by using three distinct methods. List and describe them below:

1. _____

2. _____

3. _____

The quality of a sound card is determined by the following characteristics. Explain each of the following:

Bit depth: _____
_____
_____
_____
_____

Sampling rate: _____
_____
_____
_____
_____

Feature set: _____

_____

_____

_____

_____

What is USB sound?

_____

_____

_____

_____

What are PCI sound cards?

_____

_____

_____

_____

What is built-in sound?

_____

_____

_____

_____

Sound cards are used for not only audio output, but also recording audio from a variety of external sources. While the connectivity options for sound cards vary greatly from the professional level to consumer grade, common external-audio source connections include the following:

MIDI port: _____

_____

_____

_____

Microphone-In port: _____

_____

_____

_____

Line-In port: _____

_____

_____

_____

Digital-In port: _____

_____

_____

_____

_____

What is the advantage of the Digital-In option?

_____

_____

_____

CD-ROM and DVD Drives

CDs (compact disc, read-only memory) are a popular type of removable media. Their initial use was for digital audio but it has rapidly expanded into the world of personal computer data storage. The success of CDs can be attributed to their storage capacity, ruggedness, and price. Because of the widespread acceptance of this media format, CD-ROM drives are standard devices on most personal computers.

Explain the difference between a CD-R and a CD-RW:

_____

_____

_____

_____

_____

_____

_____

What is Digital Audio Extraction (DAE) and what is it used for?

_____

_____

_____

_____

_____

_____

_____

There are two major types of CD formats, listed below. Explain each:

Logical standards: _____
_____
_____
_____
_____
_____
_____

Physical standards: _____
_____
_____
_____
_____
_____

Digital Versatile Disc (DVD) is newer technology that builds upon the strengths of CDs. DVDs share the same physical size of a CD but can handle a much greater amount of information. DVDs are used for movies, audio, and data.

Consumer demand for greater amounts of removable storage options have prompted the industry to develop methods of recording DVDs. Currently, there are four different methods of DVD recording. Each of these technologies is vying to be the standard for recordable DVD. Provide a brief explanation of each:

DVD-R: _____
_____
_____
_____

DVD-RAM: _____
_____
_____
_____

DVD-RW: _____
_____
_____
_____

DVD+RW: _____

_____

_____

_____

_____

Even though DVD and CD media share the same physical size, DVDs offer a far greater storage capacity through the use of a higher density data storing technique and through the use of layering. Explain DVD layering:

_____

_____

_____

_____

Concept Question

As a PC technician, explain the ethical considerations regarding copying CDs and copyright laws.

_____

_____

_____

_____

_____

_____

_____

_____

_____

_____

_____

_____

_____

_____

_____

_____

_____

_____

Additional Notes

_____

_____

_____

_____

_____

_____

_____

_____

_____

_____

_____

_____

_____

_____

_____

Labs and Worksheets

The following labs and worksheets are available in _CISCO NETWORKING ACADEMY PROGRAM IT Essentials I: PC Hardware and Software Lab Companion_ and as part of the online curriculum. Labs and worksheets are an excellent tool that you can use to help reinforce the material covered in this chapter.

Labs:

6.2.3   Upgrading the Video Accelerator
6.3.4   Sound Card Installation

Worksheets:

6.1.6   Multimedia Devices
6.2.5   Video Accelerators
6.3.3   Sound Cards
6.4.7   CD and DVD Terminology

A+ Exam Review Questions

The following are review questions for the A+ exam. Answers are found in Appendix A.

1. VGA stands for?
   a. Video Graphic Association
   b. Video Gradient Array
   c. Video Graphic Array
   d. Video Graphic Arrangement

2. VGA is how data is passed between the
   a. Computer and the display
   b. Display and the CD
   c. Display and the sound card
   d. Video card and the CPU

3. The number of bits that describe a pixel is known as its?
   a. Bit-resolution
   b. Bit-display
   c. Bit-technology
   d. Bit-depth

4. The actual sharpness of any particular overall display image is measured in?
   a. Dots-per-inch
   b. Pixels-per-inch
   c. Resolutions
   d. Dot pitch

5. Super VGA has a resolution of?
   a. 640 x 480
   b. 1024 x 768
   c. 800 x 900
   d. 800 x 600

6.   The basic function of the sound card is?
   a.   Input, processing, and output

   b.   Input, output, display

   c.   Processing, display, format

   d.   Display, input, format

7.   The major drawback for USB sound is?
   a.   Not compatible with Windows 98

   b.   Additional configurations are complicated

   c.   Processing power required hampers performance

   d.   Speaker system allows the USB port to act as a sound card

8.   Upgrading built-in sound requires?
   a.   Simple software

   b.   Disabling the built-in sound

   c.   Replacing the motherboard

   d.   Built-in sound cannot be upgraded

9.   What is used to select the sound card and to view its properties?
   a.   **Settings > Control Panel > System Properties > Device manager**

   b.   **Settings > Control Panel > Sounds**

   c.   **Settings > Control Panel > Add/Remove hardware**

   d.   **Explorer > Sounds**

10.   MIDI stands for?
   a.   Multiple Instrument Digital Interface

   b.   Musical Internal Digital Industry

   c.   Musical Instrument Digital Interface

   d.   Musical Instrument Direct Interface

11.   CDs are a type of?
   a.   Magnetic media

   b.   Metal media

   c.   Laser media

   d.   Optical media

12. How many methods of DVD recording are currently available?
    a.   5
    b.   3
    c.   4
    d.   2

13. A CD's logical standard determines?
    a.   Its file system structure
    b.   The amount of data that can be stored
    c.   The type of platform
    d.   The operating system

14. The difference between a laser for a CD and a laser for a DVD is?
    a.   There is no difference
    b.   The laser for the DVD must read multiple layers
    c.   The laser for the DVD is more powerful
    d.   The laser for the DVD must be faster

15. What does a video decoder circuit convert?
    a.   The digital signal into a stream of compressed signals
    b.   Compressed video
    c.   The digital signal into a stream of analog signals
    d.   The analog signal into a stream of digital signals

16. The DVD physical format defines?
    a.   The way information is stored on the DVD
    b.   The structure of the disc and the area to which data is recorded
    c.   How much data can be recorded
    d.   The number of layers allowed on the DVD

17. What is DVD5?
    a.   A single sided, single layer DVD with storage capacity up to 4.7 GB
    b.   A single sided, single layer DVD with a storage capacity of 5 GB
    c.   A double sided, double layer DVD with storage capacity up to 4.7 GB
    d.   A double sided, single layer DVD with a storage capacity of 5 GB

18.	A DVD 18 has the storage capacity of?
	a.	18 GB
	b.	180 GB
	c.	17 GB
	d.	15 GB

19.	The Y in YUV refers to the?
	a.	Luminance of the signal color
	b.	The connection port
	c.	The color component of the signal
	d.	The yellow part of the display

20.	How much throughput is required for full-motion video?
	a.	56 kbps
	b.	128 kbps
	c.	384 kbps
	d.	768 kbps

Chapter 7

Windows NT/2000/XP Operating Systems

Introduction

The Windows NT/2000 operating systems and, most recently, the Windows XP operating system have some obvious differences. Some are not so obvious at first glance. Many of the differences these operating systems have, as opposed to the 9x environments, are behind the scenes, but they are important concepts to understand to fully grasp the different environments that these operating systems are used in. For example, you must consider whether the operating system will be used for office or home and whether the computer will be part of a network. Security issues must be taken into account, and the types of programs that will be running on the operating system. All these factors determine whether or not to choose the 9x, Windows NT, 2000, or XP operating system.

This chapter focuses on the differences between the Windows NT/2000/XP operating systems and the Windows 9x operating systems. One of the biggest differences between these operating systems are the Windows NT File System (NTFS) and File Allocation Table (FAT) file systems.

What is the main purpose of the file system?

_____

_____

_____

_____

FAT File System

The original FAT file system was invented by Bill Gates in 1976. The main purpose for developing this file system was for storing programs and data on floppy disks. Basically the FAT file system is a database that keeps track of every file on the hard disk. The first company to incorporate the FAT file system design was Intel, which used it for an early version of an operating system for the Intel 8086 chip. After buying the rights to this operating system, Bill Gates rewrote it and created the first version of the Disk Operating System (DOS).

The original FAT directory structure (before Windows NT and Windows 95) limits the file names to eight characters with a three-letter extension. In addition, the FAT structure also maintains a set of attributes for each file.

Define the following file attributes?

S: _____

H: _____

A: _____

R: _____

Provide a brief description of two of the tools that the FAT 16 file system uses.

1. _____
_____
_____
_____

2. _____
_____
_____
_____

Explain clusters and sectors:

_____
_____
_____
_____
_____
_____
_____
_____
_____
_____
_____
_____

FAT32 is based on the original FAT system and works in a similar fashion to remain compatible with existing programs, networks, and device drivers. How does it differ from FAT16 and list some added features?

_____
_____
_____
_____
_____
_____
_____

NTFS was designed with the idea that the file system needs to be capable of managing global and enterprise level operating systems. The NTFS file system was designed so that it will be able to map disks up to sizes that will not even be seen in the next 20 years.

NTFS goes beyond FAT16 and FAT32 to provide support for added features such as file and directory security. Explain the following terms in relation to NTFS:

Discretionary Access Control List (DACL): _____
_____
_____
_____

System Access Control List (SACL): _____
_____
_____
_____

What is Fault Tolerance? _____
_____
_____

Security and Permissions

File and directory permissions specify which users and groups can gain access to files and folders and what they can do with the contents of the file or folder. Assigning permissions on files and directories is an excellent means of providing security and is effective whether the file or directory is being accessed over the network or from the computer itself. However, the permissions that are assigned for directories are different from the permissions assigned for files.

Define the following:

Access Control List (ACL): _____
_____
_____

Access Control Entry (ACE): _____
_____
_____

Encrypting File System (EFS): _____
_____
_____

Public Key: _____
_____
_____

Compression: _____
_____
_____

Why is compression becoming less important? _____
_____
_____
_____

Windows 2000 Boot Process

Why is it important to have a thorough understanding of the boot process?

_____
_____
_____
_____

Step One: Pre-Boot Sequence

_____
_____
_____
_____
_____

Step Two: Boot Sequence

_____
_____
_____
_____
_____

Step Three: Kernel Load

_____
_____
_____
_____
_____

Step Four: Kernel Initialization

_____
_____
_____
_____

Step Five: Logon

_____
_____
_____
_____
_____

Plug and Play

The goal of Plug and Play (PnP) is to create a computer whose hardware and software work together to automatically configure devices and assign resources, while allowing for hardware changes and additions without the need for large-scale resource assignment tweaking. As the name suggests, the user can just plug in a new device and immediately be able to use it, without complicated setup procedures.

What Windows operating system first featured PnP?

_____

The advances in PnP are significant. Why?

_____
_____
_____
_____
_____
_____
_____

What are drivers?

_____
_____
_____
_____

Define the following NTFS terms:

System tools vocabulary: _____
_____

Disk management: _____
_____

Local user account: _____
_____

Local users: _____
_____

Basic disk: _____
_____

Dynamic disk: _____
_____

Multidisk volumes: _____
_____

Simple volume: _____

_____

Spanned volume: _____

_____

Stripped volume: _____

_____

Mirrored volume: _____

_____

RAID-5 volume: _____

_____

> **NOTE** RAID used to mean arrays of inexpensive disks, which was the title of a paper written in 1988 at the University of California at Berkeley. RAIDs were contrasted with Single Large Expensive Disks (SLEDs), which were still popular on large computers. Today, all hard disks are inexpensive by comparison, and the RAID Advisory Board (www.raid-advisory.com) changed the name to independent disks several years back. (Source: TechEncyclopedia.com) Chapter 8 discusses RAID in greater detail.

Local security policy: _____

_____

Purpose of the Registry

The main components of the registry include the hardware installed on the computer, including the central processing unit (CPU), bus type, pointing device or mouse, and keyboard, device drivers, installed applications, and network adapter card settings. The registry contains a vast amount of data and is critical to how the system operates. The structure of the registry is designed to provide a secure set of records about the components that control the operating system. These components read, update, and modify data stored in the registry. List the six main components that access the registry and store data.

1. _____

2. _____

3. _____

4. _____

5. _____

6. _____

Navigating and editing the registry can be done manually using the **Regedt32.exe** command. When this command is typed, an interface is displayed that has the registry subtrees window, which allows a search through all the registry values. Subtree keys are contained within the subtrees displayed in the Registry.

Becoming familiar with these subtrees and their purpose helps to troubleshoot and maintain the computer. A key for every process that is running on a system can be found here. The following five subtrees are displayed in the Registry Editor window. Provide a description for each:

HKEY_USERS – _____
_____
_____
_____
_____

HKEY_CURRENT_CONFIG – _____
_____
_____
_____
_____

HKEY_CLASSES_ROOT – _____
_____
_____
_____
_____

HKEY_CURRENT_USER – _____
_____
_____
_____
_____

HKEY_LOCAL_MACHINE – _____
_____
_____
_____
_____

Why would a technician start the operating system in Safe Mode?

_____
_____
_____
_____

The ERD and Recovery Console for Win 2K

The systems administrator will encounter computers whose operating system have become corrupt and cannot function properly or will not even be able to boot up. Usually the problem is that a critical file or program was deleted or changed so that the operating system no longer recognizes it and therefore will no longer work. In Windows 2000 an Emergency Repair Disk (ERD) can be created or the Recovery Console feature can be used. These options help fix these problems by repairing files or copying new files that have been corrupted or damaged so that the hard drive will not have to be reformatted and lose any valuable data.

How is an ERD created in Windows?

_____

_____

_____

_____

_____

_____

_____

The Windows 2000 Recovery Console is a command-line interface that can perform a variety of troubleshooting and recovery tasks. List these tasks:

_____

_____

_____

_____

_____

_____

Explain the differences between the Windows 9x and the Windows 2000 installation:

_____

_____

_____

_____

_____

_____

_____

_____

_____

_____

What is the Hardware Abstraction Layer (HAL)?

_____

_____

_____

_____

_____

What is the benefit of setting up a system to dual boot?

_____

_____

_____

_____

_____

_____

Concept Question

As the head IT technician for a medium-sized company, you've been asked to make a presentation of the advantages and disadvantages of upgrading from Windows 98 to Windows 2000. Provide examples to help them make a decision, such as added security features and the ability to encrypt files.

_____

_____

_____

_____

_____

_____

_____

_____

_____

_____

_____

_____

_____

_____

_____

_____

_____

_____

Additional Notes

_____
_____
_____
_____
_____
_____
_____
_____
_____
_____
_____
_____
_____
_____
_____
_____
_____
_____
_____
_____
_____

Labs

The following labs are available in the CISCO NETWORKING ACADEMY PROGRAM IT
Essentials I: PC Hardware and Software Lab Companion and as part of the online
curriculum. Labs are an excellent tool that you can use to help reinforce the material
covered in this chapter.

7.1.2   Assigning Permissions in Windows 2000
7.2.1   Creating User Accounts in Windows 2000
7.2.4   Creating an Emergency Repair Disk
7.3.1   Installation Demonstration of Windows 2000

A+ Exam Review Questions

The following are review questions for the A+ exam. Answers are found in Appendix A.

1. Why is a system attribute applied to a file?
   a. So it will not be changed or deleted
   b. So it can only be read by DOS
   c. So changes to the file can be tracked
   d. So that the user knows it is a system file

2. The file system that limits the file names to eight characters is?
   a. FAT32
   b. FAT16
   c. NTFS
   d. HPFS

3. The FAT32 file system is designed to support hard drives up to?
   a. 2048 GB
   b. 512 Mb
   c. 640 MB
   d. 20 GB

4. A file system capable of managing global and enterprise level operating systems is?
   a. FAT
   b. FAT32
   c. NTFS
   d. HPFS

5. File system used by OS/2 is?
   a. FAT
   b. FAT32
   c. NTFS
   d. HPFS

6.   An advanced startup feature available for troubleshooting is?

    a.   Recovery Mode

    b.   Safe Mode

    c.   Command Mode

    d.   Help Mode

7.   The ability to restore a disk to a consistent state with minimal data loss is?

    a.   Fault Tolerance

    b.   Disk Recovery System

    c.   Disk Tolerance

    d.   Fault Recovery

8.   What does RAID stand for?

    a.   Redundant Array of Initialized Disks

    b.   Redundant Array of Information Disks

    c.   Redundant Array of Independent Disks

    d.   Redundant Array of Incorporated Disks

9.   What does POST stand for?

    a.   Pre-operating system test

    b.   Power of system test

    c.   Pre-operation self test

    d.   Power-on self test

10.   What does Plug and Play do?

    a.   Eliminates the need to manually configure jumpers on the hardware

    b.   Allows the user to plug and unplug hardware connected to the computer

    c.   Loads hardware drivers for system components

    d.   Configures GIOS information

11.   A tool that provides a list of files that a user has access to is known as?

    a.   User Access List

    b.   Administrator Access List

    c.   Access Control List

    d.   Access Control Directory

12. Users can gain access to an encrypted file if they are assigned a?
   a. Public key
   b. Password
   c. De-encryption code
   d. Administrator key

13. The NTLDR uses the following files?
   a. Ntdetect.ini, boot.ini, bootsect.ini
   b. Ntdetect.com, boot.sys, bootsect.ini
   c. Ntdetect.sys, boot.sys, bootsect.sys
   d. Ntdetect.com, boot.ini, bootsect.dos

14. A portion of a disk that functions as a physically separate unit of storage is?
   a. Partition
   b. Slave drive
   c. Cluster
   d. Sector

15. Provides a secure set of records about the components that control the OS?
   a. BIOS
   b. Registry
   c. .ini files
   d. System log

16. A library of hardware drivers that operate between the OS and hardware that is installed on the system is known as?
   a. Hardware Abstraction Layer
   b. Hardware Detail Report
   c. Library Detail Report
   d. Library Report Layer

17. A tool used before installing Windows 2000 that verifies the hardware will actually work is?
   a. Hardware Compatibility Report
   b. Hardware Comparison List
   c. Hardware Compatibility List
   d. Windows Hardware Report

18.   The Windows Compact installation option is used for?

    a.   Computer with a limited amount of hard drive space

    b.   Computer with a small tower case

    c.   Installations that need to be done quickly

    d.   Temporary installations

19.   A tool in Windows NT/2000/XP system tools that enables the administrator to control just about everything related to the local computer?

    a.   Local Tools

    b.   Administrative Tools

    c.   User Tools

    d.   Account Tools

20.   Setting up Windows to boot to 2000 or 98 is known as?

    a.   Double boot

    b.   Multi-boot

    c.   Dual boot

    d.   Semi-boot

Chapter 8

Advanced Hardware Fundamentals for Servers

Introduction

A network server is the center of a network environment. This makes the server a critical component for users to access files, e-mail, programs, printers, and so on. Because of this, fault tolerance is important for a network server. Fault tolerance is the ability for a system to continue when a hardware failure occurs. One method that provides fault tolerance is Redundant Array of Independent Disks (RAID) technology.

This chapter focuses on RAID in a network environment. It also discusses memory upgrades, the configuration of external disk subsystems, and external CD-ROM drive systems.

What is the main purpose of fault tolerance?

_____

_____

_____

_____

_____

_____

What is parity?

_____

_____

_____

_____

_____

_____

RAID

RAID is designed to allow some fault tolerance to prevent loss of data in the event of a disk drive failure on a network server. A disk drive is a mechanical device; and it is not a matter of if the disk drive will fail, but rather a matter of when the disk drive will fail. RAID accomplishes this fault tolerance or redundancy through disk drives storing parity or the same information to two different disk drives.

RAID 0

RAID 0 or simply RAID, is not RAID at all, in that it does not provide any fault tolerance (redundancy). RAID 0 is an array (or group) of disk drives used as a single disk. The data is striped or written to all the disk drives in the array. This improves disk input/output performance and speed because several chunks can be written or read simultaneously. If a disk drive in the RAID 0 array fails, all data in the RAID 0 array is lost. RAID level 0 is also often called disk striping without parity.

RAID 0 should not be used in a production server environment. Why? _____
_____
_____
_____
_____

If RAID 0 does not provide fault tolerance, why would it be implemented? _____
_____
_____
_____
_____

How many disk drives are needed to implement? _____

Advantage of RAID 0:_____
_____
_____
_____
_____

Disadvantage of RAID 0:_____
_____
_____
_____
_____

RAID 1

RAID 1 requires a minimum of two disk drives (all other RAID levels, except level 0, require at least three disk drives) to implement. RAID 1 writes all data to two separate locations. To store 20 GB of data using RAID 1, two 20-GB disk drives are required. This is a 50 percent loss of storage capacity.

RAID 1 has two different implementations: disk mirroring and disk duplexing. Explain each of these implementations:

Disk mirroring:_____
_____
_____
_____
_____

Disk duplexing:_____
_____
_____
_____
_____

Advantage of RAID 1:_____
_____
_____
_____
_____

Disadvantage of RAID 1:_____
_____
_____
_____
_____

RAID 2

RAID 2 uses a hamming code to create an Error Correcting Code (ECC) for all data to be stored on the RAID 2 array. The ECC can detect and correct single bit errors and detect double bit errors. The ECC code has to be read and decoded each time data is read from the disk. RAID 2 is difficult and expensive to implement and has a high overhead (for example, 3 parity bits for each 4 data bits).

What is a hamming code?_____
_____
_____
_____

Why isn't RAID 2 used commercially?_____
_____
_____
_____
_____

Advantage of RAID 2:_____
_____
_____
_____
_____

Disadvantage of RAID 2:_____
_____
_____
_____
_____

RAID 3

RAID 3 uses bit-level parity with a single parity disk to provide fault tolerance of data stored on the RAID 3 array in the event of failure of a single disk drive in the array. RAID 3 requires that all the disk drives in the array be synchronized with each other. The bits of the data and the parity information calculated from the data are written to all the disk drives in the array simultaneously.

What is the minimum number of disks required to implement RAID 3? _____

Advantage of RAID 3:_____

_____

_____

_____

_____

Disadvantage of RAID 3:_____

_____

_____

_____

_____

RAID 4

RAID 4 uses block-level parity with a single parity disk to provide fault tolerance to the RAID 4 array in the event of failure of a single disk drive in the array. On a RAID 4 array, data and the parity information calculated from the data is written to the disk drives in blocks; there is no need for the disk drives to be synchronized together, and the disk drives can be accessed independently.

What is the minimum number of disks required to implement RAID 4? _____

Advantage of RAID 4:_____

_____

_____

_____

_____

Disadvantage of RAID 4:_____

_____

_____

_____

_____

RAID 5

RAID 5 uses block-level parity, but spreads or stripes the parity information among all the disk drives in the disk array. This eliminates the parity drive failure common in RAID 4 systems. The loss of storage capacity in RAID 5 systems is equivalent to the storage capacity of one of the disk drives. If you have three 10-GB disk drives in a RAID 5 array, the storage capacity of the array will be 20 GB (a loss of 1/3, or 33 percent).

What is the minimum number of disks required to implement RAID 5? _____

What is a hot spare disk drive? _____
_____
_____

RAID 5 is more efficient than the other RAID levels in that the overhead is $1/n * 100$. What does the n stand for? _____

If a RAID 5 array is composed of six 18-GB disk drives, what is the overhead? Show the formula and the answer:

_____

The total storage capacity of the RAID 5 array is $(n - 1) * c$. What does the c stand for?

_____

In the same example of a RAID 5 array comprised of six 18-GB disk drives, what is the storage capacity? Show the formula and the answer:

_____

Advantage of RAID 5:_____
_____
_____
_____
_____

Disadvantage of RAID 5:_____
_____
_____
_____
_____

RAID 0/1

RAID 0/1 is also known as RAID 0+1 and it is sometimes called RAID 10. This combination of RAID gives you the best of both worlds. It will give you the performance of RAID 0 and the redundancy of RAID 1. RAID 0/1 requires at least four disk drives to implement. In RAID 0/1, there are two RAID 0 stripe sets (used to provide high input/output performance) that are mirrored (which provides the fault tolerance).

Advantage of RAID 0/1:_____
_____
_____
_____

Disadvantage of RAID 0/1:_____
_____
_____
_____

RAID Controller

RAID controllers are specialized disk controllers that use either AT Attachment (ATA) or Small Computer System Interface (SCSI) technologies. ATA RAID controllers are limited in the number of disks that can be attached because of ATA channel limitations, which are a maximum of two channels with a maximum of two disk drives per channel (for a total of four disk drives). SCSI RAID controllers have multiple channels. (Two channels are common; RAID controllers with three, four, and five channels are available.) RAID controllers are generally expensive because of the sophistication that they must contain.

List the features that should be considered when evaluating RAID controllers:

_____

_____

_____

_____

_____

Hardware RAID Versus Software RAID

RAID is usually implemented by using a RAID disk controller. However, RAID disk controllers are rather expensive. RAID can also be implemented in software by several network operating systems, including Novell NetWare, Microsoft Windows NT, and Microsoft Windows 2000.

When using the Windows 2000 version of RAID, the hard drive must be converted to a dynamic disk before the RAID options are available to implement.

Define Hardware RAID:

_____

_____

_____

_____

_____

_____

_____

Define Software RAID:

_____

_____

_____

_____

_____

_____

_____

Adding External Peripherals

External peripherals are installed to provide additional storage for the network. These external disk subsystems can be either SCSI or Fibre Channel.

How is Fibre Channel configured? _____

_____

_____

_____

_____

_____

_____

What is the Logical Unit Number (LUN) used for? _____

_____

_____

_____

_____

Processor upgrades fall into two general categories: replacing an existing processor with a faster processor, or adding an additional processor to a multiprocessor-capable network server. Whether a processor in a network server can be replaced with a faster processor depends on several factors. List these factors: _____

_____

_____

_____

_____

_____

_____

_____

_____

List the criteria required to add another processor to a multiprocessor-capable network server: _____

_____

_____

_____

_____

_____

_____

_____

How do you identify the processor that is currently installed in a system? _____

_____

_____

_____

_____

_____

_____

_____

Describe how to get the following operating systems to recognize that an additional processor has been installed on the network server:

Windows NT Server 4.0: _____

_____

_____

_____

_____

_____

_____

Windows 2000 Server: _____

_____

_____

_____

_____

_____

_____

Novell Netware 5: _____

_____

_____

_____

_____

_____

_____

Red Hat Linux: _____

_____

_____

_____

_____

_____

_____

Disk drive upgrades come in two varieties: adding disk drives to an existing network server, or replacing existing disk drives with larger or faster disk drives. Upgrades to disk drives have the most potential of any upgrade to destroy data.

What is the most important thing to do before upgrading a disk drive? _____

_____

Can an ATA drive be added to a SCSI controller? Why? _____

_____

_____

_____

It has been said that there is no such thing as too much memory in a server. Although in many cases this is true, there are a few exceptions. What is the most important consideration regarding upgrading memory in a network server? _____

_____

_____

How do you verify the current memory configuration of a network server?

_____

_____

_____

Upgrading Server Components

Define the following terms:

Video adapter onboard memory: _____

_____

_____

SCSI adapter onboard memory: _____

_____

_____

RAID controller onboard memory: _____

_____

_____

Hot replacement: _____

_____

_____

Hot upgrade: _____

_____

_____

Hot expansion: _____

_____

_____

What are system monitoring agents? _____

_____

_____

Concept Question

Explain the differences between hardware- and software-based RAID and provide examples where you would use hardware RAID and software RAID for optimal performance.

_____
_____
_____
_____
_____
_____
_____
_____
_____
_____
_____
_____
_____
_____
_____
_____
_____
_____
_____

Additional Notes

_____
_____
_____
_____
_____
_____
_____
_____
_____
_____
_____
_____
_____
_____
_____
_____
_____

Labs and Worksheets

The following labs and worksheets are available in *Cisco Networking Academy Program IT Essentials I: PC Hardware and Software Lab Companion* and as part of the online curriculum. Labs and worksheets are an excellent tool that you can use to help reinforce the material covered in this chapter.

Labs:

8.1.2   Basic Disk to Dynamic Disk Conversion

Worksheets:

8.1.3   RAID
8.4.3   Adding Processors
8.5.3   Adapters

A+ Exam Review Questions

The following are review questions for the A+ exam. Answers are found in Appendix A.

1.   The ability for a system to continue when a hardware failure occurs is?
    a.   Failure tolerance

    b.   Hardware tolerance

    c.   Fault recovery

    d.   Fault tolerance

2.   A device that connects one keyboard, one mouse, and one monitor to two or more computers is called?
    a.   KVM

    b.   KVV

    c.   MVK

    d.   KMM

3.   Which RAID should not be used in a production server environment?
    a.   RAID 1

    b.   RAID 2

    c.   RAID 0

    d.   RAID 4

4.   Two disk drives that are connected to the same disk controller is?
    a.   Device mirroring

    b.   Disk mirroring

    c.   Disk duplexing

    d.   Drive duplexing

5.   Each disk drive in a mirrored set is connected to a different disk controller is?
    a.   Device mirroring

    b.   Disk mirroring

    c.   Disk duplexing

    d.   Drive duplexing

6. An array or group of disk drives used as a single disk that does not provide any redundancy is?

   a. RAID 0

   b. RAID 1

   c. RAID 2

   d. RAID 4

7. Uses bit-level parity with a single parity disk to provide fault tolerance of the data stored?

   a. RAID 0

   b. RAID 1

   c. RAID 2

   d. RAID 3

8. Writes all data to two separate locations?

   a. RAID 0

   b. RAID 1

   c. RAID 2

   d. RAID 5

9. What does ECC stand for?

   a. Error Correcting Code

   b. Error Code Combination

   c. Emergency Correcting Code

   d. Error Combination Coding

10. Type of RAID that uses a hamming code to create ECC for all data to be stored?

    a. RAID 4

    b. RAID 1

    c. RAID 2

    d. RAID 3

11. Type of RAID that uses block-level parity with a single parity disk to provide fault tolerance?

    a. RAID 4

    b. RAID 5

    c. RAID 2

    d. RAID 3

12. Type of RAID that uses block-level parity but spreads the parity information among all the disk drives in the array?

   a.   RAID 4

   b.   RAID 1

   c.   RAID 5

   d.   RAID 3

13. A RAID controller that limits the number of disks that can be used?

   a.   ATA RAID controller

   b.   SCSI RAID controller

   c.   BUS controller

   d.   System controller

14. When using the Windows 2000 version of software RAID, the hard drive must be?

   a.   Converted to system disk

   b.   Formatted

   c.   Converted to basic disk

   d.   Converted to dynamic disk

15. CD-ROM drive libraries are implemented to?

   a.   Provide CD storage

   b.   Accommodate CD-ROM drives for client computers on the network

   c.   Provide additional processing power to the RAID controller

   d.   Allow users to check out and try different software

16. What does LUN stand for?

   a.   Logical Unit Number

   b.   Logical Unit Network

   c.   Leading Unit Number

   d.   Linux Unit Network

17. The most important factor to consider when deciding whether a processor in a network server can be upgraded with a faster processor is?

   a.   Is the server room cool enough

   b.   Are there enough hard drives

   c.   Can the memory cache support the faster clock speed

   d.   Will the motherboard support it

18. What does HAL stand for?

    a. Hardware Allowance Level

    b. Hardware Abstraction Layer

    c. Hardware Abstraction Level

    d. Hardware Absence Layer

19. Technology that allows you to replace, upgrade, or add an adapter without powering down the network server is?

    a. Hot Swappable

    b. PCI Quick Plug

    c. BIOS Replace

    d. Hot Components

20. What two common metals are used on the memory module leads and the connectors in the memory slots?

    a. Gold and silver

    b. Tin and copper

    c. Tin and gold

    d. Silver and copper

Chapter 9

Networking Fundamentals

Introduction

A network is a connected system of objects or people. The most common example of a network is the telephone system, which is widely known as the Public Switched Telephone Network (PSTN). The PSTN allows people in virtually every corner of the world to communicate with anyone who has access to a telephone.

In a similar fashion, a computer network allows users to communicate with other users on the same network by transmitting data on the cables that connect them. A computer network is defined as having two or more devices (such as workstations, printers, or servers) that are linked together for the purpose of sharing information, resources, or both. The link can be made through a variety of copper or fiber-optic cables or it can be a wireless connection that uses radio signals, infrared technology (laser), or even satellite transmission. The information and resources shared on a network can include data files, application programs, printers, modems, or other hardware devices. Computer networks are used in businesses, schools, government agencies, and even some homes.

This chapter details the types of networks, the topology of networks, and the Open Systems Interconnection (OSI) model. It is important to understand that networks are multi-layered. A network consists of many overlapping systems, such as cabling, addressing schemes, or applications. The layers work together to transmit and receive data. The OSI model was created to define these multiple layers.

The Benefits of Networking

Regardless of the size of the network, the benefits are the same. List three major reasons to implement a network:

1. _____

   _____

2. _____

   _____

3. _____

   _____

The data channels over which a signal is sent can operate in one of three ways: simplex, half-duplex, or full-duplex (often just called duplex). The distinction is in the way that the signal can travel. Explain each:

Simplex: _____
_____
_____

Half-duplex:_____
_____
_____

Full-duplex:_____
_____
_____

Types of Networks

By using local-area network (LAN) and wide-area network (WAN) technologies, many computers are interconnected to provide services to their users. In providing services, networked computers take on different roles or functions in relation to each other. Some types of applications require computers to function as equal partners.

Other types of applications distribute work so that one computer functions to serve a number of others in an unequal relationship. In either case, two computers typically communicate with each other by using request/response protocols. One computer issues a request for a service, and a second computer receives and responds to that request. The requester takes on the role of a client, and the responder takes on the role of a server.

The type of network where computers act as equal partners and individuals control their own resources is known as _____

The type of network where one computer functions to respond to the requests of clients is known as _____

Starting in the late 1960s and early 1970s, network engineers designed a form of network that enabled many computers in a small area to share a single communications channel by taking turns using it. This network is known as a _____
_____

A network that connects computers over long distances is known as _____
_____

What is a circuit-switched network?

_____

_____

_____

_____

What is a packet-switched network?

_____

_____

_____

_____

Adding a Network Interface Card

A network interface card (NIC) is a device that plugs into a motherboard and provides the port for the network cable connection. It is the computer's interface with the LAN. The NIC communicates with the network through serial connections and communicates with the computer through parallel connections. When a NIC is installed in a computer, it requires an interrupt request line (IRQ), an Input/Output (I/O) address, and memory space for the operating system drivers.

List the three important considerations to bear in mind when selecting a NIC to use on a network:

1. _____

2. _____

3. _____

In a Transmission Control Protocol/Internet Protocol (TCP/IP)-based LAN, PCs use IP addresses to identify each other. These addresses allow computers that are attached to the network to locate each other. An IP address is a 32-bit binary number. This binary number is divided into four groups of eight bits known as octets, each of which is represented by a decimal number in the range of 0 to 255. The octets are separated by decimal points. The combination 190.100.5.54 is an example of an IP address. This type of address is described as a dotted decimal representation. Each device on the network that has an IP address is known as a host or node.

Although IP addresses can be set manually, the most common and efficient way is through a Dynamic Host Configuration Protocol (DHCP). How does the DHCP work?

_____

_____

_____

_____

_____

What is a default gateway?

_____

_____

_____

_____

_____

The Domain Name System (DNS) translates computer names such as cisco.com to their corresponding unique IP address. Why is this important?

_____

_____

_____

_____

_____

Network Topologies

The network topology defines the way in which computers, printers, and other devices are connected. A network topology describes the layout of the wire and devices and the paths used by data transmissions. The topology greatly influences how the network functions.

On the lines below, enter the name of each topology pictured and describe where it would best be used:

_____

_____

_____

_____

_____

_____

_____

126

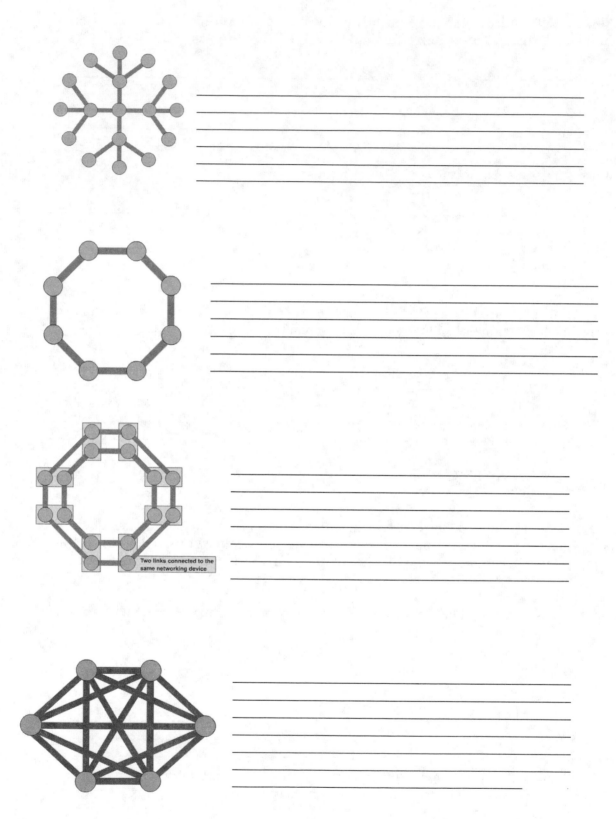

Two links connected to the
same networking device

_____
_____
_____
_____
_____
_____

_____
_____
_____
_____
_____
_____

_____
_____
_____
_____
_____
_____
_____
_____

_____
_____
_____
_____
_____
_____
_____
_____

Networking Media Vocabulary

Networking media can be defined simply as the means by which signals (data) are sent from one computer to another (either by cable or wireless means). There are a wide variety of networking media in the marketplace including two that use copper (coaxial and twisted-pair), one that uses glass (fiber-optic), and one that uses waves (wireless) to transmit data.

Write a brief description for each of the network media terms:

Coaxial cable: _____
_____
_____

Twisted pair: _____
_____
_____

Shielded twisted pair: _____
_____
_____

Unshielded twisted pair: _____
_____
_____

RS-232: _____
_____
_____

Fiber-optic cable: _____
_____
_____

Wireless: _____
_____
_____

Common Networking Devices

Networking devices connect computers and peripheral devices so that they can communicate.

Explain the following devices used in a network environment:

Hub: _____
_____
_____

Bridges: _____
_____
_____

Switches: _____
_____
_____

Routers: _____
_____
_____

Server Components

Server components are those components that are used exclusively with the network server. End users depend on the server to provide the services required. To keep the server running at it's optimal performance, a higher level of preventive maintenance must be maintained.

What is a KVM and what is it used for? _____
_____
_____
_____

What is the purpose of a redundant NIC? _____
_____
_____
_____

The layout of the server rack is important. What are some of the considerations for how components should be installed? _____
_____
_____
_____

Ethernet

The Ethernet architecture is now the most popular type of LAN architecture. Architecture refers to the overall structure of a computer or communication system. It determines the capabilities and limitations of the system. The Ethernet architecture is based on the IEEE 802.3 standard. The IEEE 802.3 standard specifies that a network implement the Carrier Sense Multiple Access with Collision Detection (CSMA/CD) access control method. CSMA/CD uses baseband transmission over coaxial or twisted-pair cable that is laid out in a bus topology (a linear or star bus). Standard transfer rates are 10 Mbps or 100 Mbps, but new standards provide for gigabit Ethernet, which is capable of attaining speeds up to 1 Gbps over fiber-optic cable or other high-speed media.

10BaseT

Currently 10BaseT is one of the most popular Ethernet implementations. It uses a star topology. The 10 stands for the common transmission speed 10 Mbps, the "Base is for baseband mode, and the T stands for twisted pair cabling. The term Ethernet cable describes the unshielded twisted-pair (UTP) cabling that is generally used in this architecture. Shielded twisted-pair (STP) also can be used. 10BaseT and its cousin, 100BaseX, make networks that are easy to set up and expand.

List the advantages of 10BaseT:

_____
_____
_____
_____

List the disadvantages of 10BaseT:

_____
_____
_____
_____

100BaseX

100BaseX comes in several different varieties. It can be implemented over 4-pair Category 3, 4, or 5 UTP (100BaseT). It can also be implemented over 2-pair Category 5 UTP or STP (100BaseTX), or as Ethernet over 2-strand fiber-optic cable (100BaseFX).

List the advantages of 100BaseX:

_____

_____

_____

_____

List the disadvantages of 100BaseX:

_____

_____

_____

_____

1000BaseT

If 100BaseX is known as Fast Ethernet, 1000BaseT must be considered a speed demon. Its common nickname is Gigabit Ethernet. Although not yet in widespread implementation in production networks, this architecture supports data transfer rates of 1 Gbps, which is remarkably fast. Gigabit Ethernet is, for the most part, a LAN architecture although its implementation over fiber-optic cable makes it suitable for metropolitan-area networks (MANs).

List the advantages of 1000BaseX:

_____

_____

_____

_____

List the sisadvantages of 1000BaseX:

_____

_____

_____

_____

Token Ring

Token Ring is so named because of its logical topology and its media access control method of token passing. The transfer rate for Token Ring can be either 4 Mbps or 16 Mbps.

Token Ring is a baseband architecture that uses digital signaling. In that way it resembles Ethernet, but the communication process is quite different in many respects. Token Ring is an active topology. As the signal travels around the circle to each network card, it is regenerated before being sent on its way.

Explain the term hall monitor:

_____

_____

_____

_____

What determines the direction of data travel in a token ring?

_____

_____

FDDI

Fiber Distributed Data Interface (FDDI) is a type of Token Ring network. Its implementation and topology differ from the IBM Token Ring LAN architecture, which IEEE 802.5 governs. FDDI is often used for MANs or larger LANs, such as those connecting several buildings in an office complex or campus. MANs typically span a metro area.

As its name implies, FDDI runs on fiber-optic cable, and thus combines high-speed performance with the advantages of the token-passing ring topology. FDDI runs at 100 Mbps, and its topology is a dual ring. The outer ring is called the primary ring and the inner ring is called the secondary ring.

Computers on a FDDI network are divided into two classes:

1. _____

2. _____

Advantages of FDDI:

_____

_____

_____

Disadvantages of FDDI:

_____

_____

_____

OSI Model

The OSI reference model is an industry standard framework that divides the functions of networking into seven distinct layers. It is one of the most commonly used teaching and reference tools. The International Organization for Standardization (ISO, not to be confused with OSI) developed the OSI model in the 1980s.

There are seven layers in the OSI reference model. Each layer provides specific services to the layers above and below it for the network to work effectively.

At the top of the model is the application interface (layer), which enables the smooth usage of such applications as word processors and Web browsers.

At the bottom is the physical side of the network. The physical side includes the cabling, NIC, hubs, and other networking hardware.

Provide the purpose of each of the layers of the OSI model in the table below:

Layer #	Layer Name	PDU	Purpose
7	Application	Data	
6	Presentation	Data	
5	Session	Data	
4	Transport	Segment	
3	Network	Packet	
2	Data-link	Frame	
1	Physical	Bits	

A mnemonic will help you remember the seven layers of the OSI: "All People Seem To Like Data Processing," or "Please Do Not Throw Sausage Pizza Away."

Briefly describe how the OSI model works?

_____
_____
_____
_____
_____
_____
_____
_____
_____
_____

What is a protocol?

_____
_____
_____
_____
_____
_____
_____
_____

TCP/IP Utilities

TCP/IP is a complex collection of protocols. Most vendors implement the suite to include a variety of utilities for viewing configuration information and troubleshooting problems.

Provide a brief explanation of the following utilities:

Ping: _____
_____
_____

ARP: _____
_____
_____

RARP: _____
_____
_____

NSLOOKUP.EXE: _____
_____
_____

Netstat/Tpcon: _____
_____
_____

Nbtstat: _____
_____
_____

Ipconfig: _____
_____
_____

Winipcfg: _____
_____
_____

Config: _____
_____
_____

Ifconfig: _____
_____
_____

Tracert: _____
_____
_____

Iptrace: _____
_____
_____

Traceroute: _____
_____
_____

Connecting to the Internet

Serial lines that are established over serial cabling connect to one of a computer's standard RS-232 communication (COM) ports. Serial transmission sends data one bit at a time. Analog or digital signals depend on changes in the state (modulations) to represent the actual binary data. To correctly interpret the signals, the receiving network device must know precisely when to measure the signal. Therefore, timing becomes important in networking. In fact, the biggest problem with sending data over serial lines is keeping the transmitted data bit timing coordinated. Provide a brief description of the two techniques that provide proper timing for serial transfers:

Synchronous serial transmission:_____

_____

_____

_____

_____

_____

Asynchronous serial transmission: _____

_____

_____

_____

_____

_____

The modem is an electronic device that is used for computer communications through telephone lines. It allows data transfer between one computer and another. The Universal Asynchronous Receiver/Transmitter (UART) converts byte-oriented data to serial bit streams. Blocks of data are handled by software. Internal modems combine a UART and a modem on board. The modems convert digital data to analog signals and analog signals back to digital data.

The term modem actually derives from the device's function. The process of converting analog signals to digital and back again is called **mo**dulation/**dem**odulation (hence the term modem). Modem-based transmission is remarkably accurate, despite the fact that telephone lines can be quite noisy because of clicks, static, and other problems.

Name/list the four main types of modems:

1._____

2._____

3._____

4._____

The modem must operate in two states in order to enable dial-up networking (DUN). Please name these two states:

1._____

2._____

What is handshaking? _____
_____
_____
_____

What are AT commands? _____
_____
_____
_____

What is an ISP? _____
_____
_____
_____

Digital Subscriber Line (DSL) is an always-on technology. This means that there is no need to dial up each time to connect to the Internet. It is a relatively new technology currently being offered by phone companies as an add-on service over existing copper wire or phone lines. List the five available DSL services:

1. _____

2. _____

3. _____

4. _____

5. _____

What are the advantages of DSL?_____
_____
_____
_____
_____
_____
_____
_____
_____
_____

What are the disadvantages of DSL?_____

_____
_____
_____
_____
_____
_____
_____
_____
_____
_____

A cable modem acts like a LAN interface by connecting a computer to the Internet. The cable modem connects a computer to the cable company's network through the same coaxial cabling that feeds cable TV (CATV) signals to a television set. Generally, cable modems are designed to provide Internet access only, whereas analog modems or ISDN adapters allow dial-in to any service provider or service in a remote access server. With a cable modem, the cable company must be used.

What are the advantages of cable modems?_____

_____
_____
_____
_____
_____
_____
_____
_____
_____

What are the disadvantages of cable modems?_____

_____
_____
_____
_____
_____
_____
_____
_____
_____
_____

Concept Question

A company with about 500 employees is ready to get a network up and running. They are located in two different offices in two different cities. Use the space below to describe the type of network that will provide the file sharing they need and their link to the Internet.

_____
_____
_____
_____
_____
_____
_____
_____
_____
_____
_____
_____

Display a topology graphic for the network designed.

Additional Notes

_____
_____
_____
_____
_____
_____
_____
_____
_____
_____
_____
_____
_____
_____
_____
_____
_____
_____
_____
_____
_____
_____
_____

Labs and Worksheets

The following labs and worksheets are available in the _CISCO NETWORKING ACADEMY PROGRAM IT Essentials I: PC Hardware and Software Lab Companion_ and as part of the online curriculum. Labs and worksheets are an excellent tool that you can use to help reinforce the material covered in this chapter.

Labs:
9.3.1   NIC Installation
9.3.3   Configuring the NIC to Work with a DHCP Server
9.7.2   Troubleshooting a NIC Using the Ping Command
Worksheets:
9.2.5   Types of Networks
9.4.2   Network Topology
9.6.5   OSI Model, TCP/IP, Protocols
9.8.7   Connecting to the Internet

A+ Exam Review Questions

The following are review questions for the A+ exam. Answers are found in Appendix A.

1. The largest network of computers in the world is called the?
    a.   DoD
    b.   World Wide Web
    c.   Internet
    d.   Microsoft

2. When was the Internet developed?
    a.   Late 1950
    b.   Late 1960
    c.   Late 1970
    d.   Late 1980

3. When you have three computers sharing communications, it is known as a?
    a.   Operating system
    b.   Network
    c.   Remote connection
    d.   Sharing violation

4. How do you share a resource on the network in Windows 98 using the Windows Explorer?
    a.   Highlight the desired item then right-click and select **Explore**
    b.   Highlight the desired item then right-click and select **Open**
    c.   Highlight the desired item then right-click and select **Network**
    d.   Highlight the desired item then right-click and select **Sharing**

5. What is the problem if other computers on the network cannot see files or printers on your computer?
    a.   The printer driver is outdated
    b.   The Internet connection is too slow
    c.   Their network settings are incorrect
    d.   File and print sharing was not enabled

6. To set up remote administration, which object would you select?

   a. RAS

   b. Passwords

   c. Dial-up networking

   d. NAT

7. A controlled sequence of messages that are exchanged between two or more systems to accomplish a given task is called a?

   a. Protocol

   b. TCP

   c. LAN

   d. ISP

8. Which of the following is not a basic network architecture?

   a. Extended star

   b. Ring

   c. Extended ring

   d. Star

9. What does NIC stand for?

   a. No Information Current

   b. Network Interface Card

   c. Network Internet Community

   d. Network Isolation Committee

10. What does DNS provide?

    a. It maps e-mail messages to routers

    b. It maps IP addresses to names

    c. Distributes IP addresses

    d. Web browsers

11. What is the best way to keep a network server cool?

    a. Air conditioning

    b. Cooling fan

    c. Perforations on the doors and the sides

    d. All of the above

12. What is the standard Internet addressing scheme that creates the linkage between sub-networks called?

    a. Internet address

    b. IP address

    c. Web address

    d. MAC address

13. If you are using a Token Ring network, when does each station transmit?

    a. When no other stations are using the network

    b. Only when that station has been given transmission time

    c. Only when the station processes the Token

    d. Only when another station on the network permits

14. A UTP cable has?

    a. Two pairs of two twisted wires

    b. Four pairs of twisted wires

    c. Four sets of four wires

    d. Two pairs of four twisted wires

15. A cable with a braided copper shield around it and only a single conductor is known as?

    a. UTP

    b. STP

    c. FDDI

    d. Coax

16. In a twisted pair network, what type of conductor is used?

    a. 100Base2

    b. 10Base2

    c. 10BaseT

    d. 10BaseFL

17. What do you do if you PING an IP address and cannot get a response?

    a. Use the **tracert** command

    b. Use the MSD command

    c. Try a different IP address

    d. Ask the site when it will be running

18. How many layers does the OSI reference model have?
   a. Six
   b. Seven
   c. Eight
   d. Nine

19. Which layer of the OSI model describes the cable and how it is attached?
   a. Network
   b. Transport
   c. Data-link
   d. Physical

20. Which layer of the OSI model is responsible for establishing a unique network address?
   a. Network
   b. Transport
   c. Data-link
   d. Physical

21. Which layer of the OSI model is responsible for the accuracy of the data transmission?
   a. Presentation
   b. Data-link
   c. Session
   d. Transport

22. Which layer of the OSI model translates data into an appropriate transmission format?
   a. Application
   b. Network
   c. Presentation
   d. Data-link

23. To receive access to the Internet, which network protocol is required?
   a. TCP/IP
   b. ISP
   c. OPX/SPX Novellware
   d. DNS

24. Data bits that are sent without a synchronizing clock pulse are called?
    a. Synchronous
    b. Asynchronous
    c. Dial-up
    d. Sequential

25. To receive a direct connection to the Internet, what is required?
    a. At least two routers between the local network and the Internet
    b. Only a bridge between the local network and the Internet
    c. Only a hub between the local network and the Internet
    d. Only one router between the local network and the Internet

Chapter 10

Printers

Introduction

Printers are a vital part of modern PC systems. The need for hard copies of computer and online documents is no less important today than when the paperless revolution began several years ago. Today's computer technician must be able to understand the operation of various types of printers to install, maintain, and troubleshoot printer problems. This chapter details the different types of printers, maintenance, and the management of printers in a network environment.

The most popular types of printers in use are electrophotographic type laser printers, sprayed inkjet printers, and impact type dot matrix printers. Several older types of impact printers such as the daisy wheel are seldom used.

Printers are connected to personal computers with serial, parallel, and network cable connections. Wireless types of connections include infrared and radio wave technology.

Printer drivers are software that must be installed on the PC so that the printer can communicate and coordinate the printing process. Printer drivers vary according to printer type, manufacturer, and model.

Safety Procedures

It is extremely important to follow all safety procedures when working with printers. Parts can become very hot, for example, the fuser on the laser printer and the print head on a dot matrix printer.

The voltage device that is used to erase the drum of a laser printer (called the primary corona wire or grid, or the conditioning roller, is dangerous. This voltage runs as high as 6000 DC volts.

Before performing any maintenance on any type of printer, make sure the power is off.

Types of Printers

The dot matrix printer belongs to a printer class called impact printers. In this type, the printing part actually impacts a printer tape or inked ribbon to cause characters to be formed on paper.

What determines the quality of print for a dot matrix printer? _____
_____

What does NLQ stand for and what does it mean? _____
_____

What type of paper is most used with the dot matrix printer? _____
_____

Color inkjet printers are the most popular type of printer in home use today. This is because of their low cost and moderate quality of print. The inkjet printer uses liquid ink-filled cartridges that force out and spray ink particles at the page through tiny holes called nozzles. Although inkjet printers usually print one page at a time, they are still faster than the dot matrix printer.

The inkjet printer sprays tiny dots of ink at the page by applying pressure that is caused by electricity or an electrical charge. Pressure inside the ink reservoir of the cartridge is less than the outside pressure until the electricity is applied, then the pressure rises. This internal pressure causes small dots of ink to be forced out through the nozzles.

Inkjet printers have two kinds of print heads. List them and describe how they operate:

_____
_____
_____
_____

_____
_____
_____
_____

How is the quality of print measured? _____

How is the speed measured? _____

What type of paper is used most? _____Today, the laser printer is the printer of preference because of its high resolution, superior operation, and speed. However, its internal operation is more complex than other types of printers, which makes it the most costly printer choice.

As in photocopiers, static electricity is the primary principle that is used in the operation of a laser printer. This is the same static electricity that causes lightning or other oppositely charged particles to attract each other. This attraction is used to temporally hold small dry ink particles called toner to a statically charged image on an electrophotographic drum. A laser beam is used to draw this image.

Define temporal as it relates to statically charged toner:_____
_____
_____

The central part of the laser printer is its electrophotographic drum. The drum is a metal cylinder that is coated with a light sensitive insulating material. When a beam of laser light strikes the drum, it becomes a conductor at the point where the light hits it. As the drum rotates, the laser beam draws an electrostatic image upon the drum called the image.

The latent image, that is the undeveloped image, is passed by a supply of dry ink or toner that is attracted to it. The drum turns and brings this image in contact with the paper, which attracts the toner from the drum. The paper is passed through a fuser that is made up of hot rollers which melts the toner into the paper.

Provide a brief explanation for each of the six steps in the laser printing:

Cleaning: _____
_____
_____
_____

Conditioning: _____
_____
_____
_____

Writing: _____
_____
_____
_____

Developing: _____
_____
_____
_____

Transferring: _____
_____
_____
_____

Fusing: _____
_____
_____
_____

A good way to memorize the order of steps for certification is using the first letter from each word to create a mnemonic: <u>C</u>ontinuous <u>C</u>are <u>W</u>ill <u>D</u>elay <u>T</u>rouble <u>F</u>orever.

Can you think of another mnemonic? _____

_____

What part of the laser printer should never be exposed to light for long periods of time?

_____

Buying a Printer

Speed and capacity are important factors in printing. These are even more important if the printer is to be used in a fast-pace work environment.

In addition, quality of print must be considered and the resolution. Resolution refers to the number of tiny dots the print head is capable of fitting per inch when forming an image. The printer must be reliable regardless of the environment, and the related costs should be considered.

The cost for cartridges, toner, replacement parts, paper, and so on, adds up to the total cost of ownership (TCO).

Indicate which printer might be selected for the following environments:

Home office: _____

Small office: _____

Medium-sized office: _____

Large corporation: _____

Printers require a method of communicating with the computers they serve. Communication is accomplished through the ports on both the printer and the computer (or network device) or by using wireless technologies (such as infrared signals). Most printers use serial, parallel, Universal Serial Bus (USB), Small Computer System Interface (SCSI), and network cables and ports to receive information from computers.

Provide a brief description of each of the following connections:

Serial: _____

_____

_____

_____

Parallel: _____
_____
_____
_____

SCSI: _____
_____
_____
_____

USB: _____
_____
_____
_____

FireWire: _____
_____
_____
_____

Network:_____
_____
_____
_____

Infrared: _____
_____
_____
_____

What is PDL? _____
_____
_____

What is WYSIWYG? _____
_____
_____

List today's most popular PDLs:

_____

_____

_____

What is a print driver? _____
_____
_____
_____
_____

Where would you find the most current print driver? _____
_____
_____
_____

Maintenance

Printers, especially in large corporations, require regular maintenance to keep them running efficiently. Describe the steps to perform the following maintenance routines:

Ink and toner installation and replacement: _____
_____
_____
_____
_____
_____

Print media installation and adjustment: _____
_____
_____
_____
_____
_____

Installing additional memory: _____
_____
_____
_____
_____
_____

Adding a Local Printer

Adding a local printer is a relatively easy process. Describe the steps to accomplish this task:

_____
_____
_____
_____
_____
_____
_____

How do you verify that the printer has been installed properly?

_____

When a computer sends a document to a printer for output, the information must be translated from the operating system's format to the PDL of the printer. The PDL then creates a raster (bitmap) image of the document, and the printer outputs the image. These language translations and the drawing of the raster image can be time consuming.

How does the use of host-based printing speed up print jobs? _____
_____
_____
_____
_____

What device enables a computer to print to different printers or output devices? _____
_____
_____

Fonts

A font is a complete set of characters of a particular typeface used for display and printing purposes. These characters include letters, numbers, and other symbols that share a common theme or look. Fonts can be modified by size, weight, and style. Groups of fonts with differing styles are called font families. Display fonts are used for screen output, and print fonts are used for hardcopy output. Display fonts and print fonts try to match one another as closely as possible to ensure that the user has true WYSIWYG output. When using host-based printing technology, virtually any font that can be displayed on the screen can be output to the printer, but using true print fonts can speed up the printing process even more.

Describe the two varieties of print fonts:

_____

_____

_____

_____

_____

_____

Configuring Printer Sharing

Sharing resources, like printers, was one of the reasons networks were developed. A group of users sharing a single printer is far more economical than buying each user an individual printer.

What adaptor is required for a printer to connect to a printer? _____

What is a print server? _____

_____

_____

Most network operating systems have their own utilities to set up printers. In Windows, this is called: _____

Explain the differences between adding a local printer and adding a network printer:

_____

_____

_____

_____

Managing a Printer

Many users, all with different levels of security, access printers in a high volume environment. It is important that managing the printer queue is restricted to just a few individuals such as the network administrator and print server administrator.

What is a printer queue? _____

_____

_____

_____

The network administrator can then determine the priority of users and print jobs. For example, the network administrator can prioritize all print jobs from the president and vice-presidents of the company or from the accounting department.

In addition, the following tasks can be performed:

_____
_____
_____

How is a default printer selected? _____

_____
_____

What is media? _____

_____

Each model of printer can have its own set of unique user-selectable options. The two main categories of printer options are media handling and printer output.

In general, media handling options set the way a printer handles the media. This can include input paper tray selection, output path selection, media size and orientation and paper weight selection.

Printer output options deal with how the ink or toner is placed on the media. Color management, print quality, and print speed are common printer output options.

Although some printer options can be selected through physical switches located on the printer, most of today's printer options are configured through the printer driver.

Describe the two methods of selecting individual printer options:

Global method: _____

_____
_____
_____
_____

Per-document method: _____

_____
_____
_____
_____

Concept Question

The company where you work has ten laser printers and two color printers networked. They have asked you to talk to the users about how to access the appropriate printer for the specific print job, troubleshooting problems that can occur, and why you are concerned about the weather. The forecast calls for high humidity. They need to know the type of problems a user can fix and the type of problems that require a technician.

_____
_____
_____
_____
_____
_____
_____
_____
_____
_____
_____
_____
_____
_____
_____
_____
_____
_____

Additional Notes

_____
_____
_____
_____
_____
_____
_____
_____
_____
_____
_____
_____
_____

Labs and Worksheets

The following labs and worksheets are available in the *CISCO NETWORKING ACADEMY PROGRAM IT Essentials I: PC Hardware and Software Lab Companion* and as part of the online curriculum. Labs and worksheets are an excellent tool that you can use to help reinforce the material covered in this chapter.

Labs
10.3.8 Adding an Ink Jet Printer to Your Computer
10.4.4 Setting up Print Sharing Capabilities
10.5.4 Managing Files in a Printer Queue
Worksheet
10.6.1 Paper Jams

A+ Exam Review Questions

The following are review questions for the A+ exam. Answers are found in Appendix A.

1. What is the most likely problem when a dot matrix printer has a light printout?
    a. Worn print head
    b. Worn platen
    c. Used ribbon
    d. Empty ink cartridge

2. How many pins do print heads have on a dot matrix printer?
    a. 9-pin or 24-pin
    b. 9-pin or 28-pin
    c. 7-pin or 24-pin
    d. 7-pin or 28-pin

3. Which part of a dot matrix printer will produce a burn if touched?
    a. The platen
    b. The rollers
    c. The print head cable
    d. The print head

4. What component of a dot matrix printer should not be lubricated?
    a. The head transport rails
    b. Shafts and gears
    c. The bearings of the platen
    d. The pins in the print head

5. Which of the following is non-impact?
    a. Dot matrix printer
    b. Inkjet printer
    c. Daisy wheel
    d. Feed printer

6. What type of printer forces ink through a nozzle with a piezo-electric crystal to print?
   a. Laser printer
   b. Dot matrix
   c. Inkjet
   d. A plotter

7. When an inkjet printer has completed a print job, the paper is?
   a. Often still wet
   b. Very hot
   c. Charged with electrostatic particles
   d. Has a uniform positive charge

8. The quality of print for an inkjet printer is measured in?
   a. rpm
   b. dpi
   c. kps
   d. lpi

9. The thermal fuse in a laser printer prevents?
   a. Corona failure
   b. The fuser from overheating
   c. The power supply from overheating
   d. The drum from overheating

10. What does the primary corona of a laserjet printer do?
    a. Applies a uniform positive charge to the drum
    b. Applies a uniform negative charge to the drum
    c. Removes a uniform positive charge from the drum
    d. Removes a uniform negative charge from the drum

11. In a laser printer, what do you use to clean the primary corona wire?
    a. Lint-free cloth dampened with cold demineralized water
    b. Lint-free cloth dampened with deionized water
    c. A dry, lint-free cloth
    d. Lint-free cloth dampened with denatured alcohol

12. What comes between the conditioning phase and the developing phase in the laser printing process?
   a. Charging phase
   b. Writing phase
   c. Fusing phase
   d. Cleaning phase

13. What are command and control languages most commonly associated with printers?
   a. PCL and PostScript
   b. PPP and PC Script
   c. Electrophotographic and PCL
   d. PCL and PPP

14. A cable with a 9-pin male connector at one end and a 9-pin female connector at the other end is?
   a. Mouse extension cable
   b. Serial port cable
   c. Parallel port cable
   d. Monitor cable

15. What kind of font is True Type?
   a. An interface font
   b. A bit-mapped font
   c. A vector-based font
   d. A narrow font

16. How do you open the print queue in Windows 98?
   a. Click the printer **Post Script** icon
   b. Open the **Print Queue** folder under My Computer
   c. Under **File** where the document was created
   d. Click the desired printer in the **Printer** folder

17. How do you reorder a print job in a print queue in Windows 98?
   a. Drag and drop it to the **Start > Print > Top Queue** icon
   b. It is not possible
   c. Drag and drop it to the desired position in the queue
   d. Use the Print Order menu under My Computer

18. What is the first thing to do when troubleshooting a printer problem?

   a. Check the power and paper

   b. Check for IRQ conflicts

   c. Re-install the print driver

   d. Remove the ink cartridge or toner cartridge and re-install

19. What does Windows 98 use to make printer setup easier?

   a. Queue support

   b. Plug and Play support

   c. Updated printer support

   d. Port support

20. The majority of printer problems are because of?

   a. Paper jams

   b. Toner units

   c. Stripped gears

   d. Defective rollers

Chapter 11

Preventive Maintenance

The goal of preventive maintenance is to avoid problems. This chapter addresses the steps required to maintain computer components and a network server. A preventive maintenance program should be developed for the following reasons:

- Preventive maintenance saves money

- Preventive maintenance saves time

- Preventive maintenance helps safeguard important data

- Preventive maintenance improves performance

Equally important to the tasks of preventive maintenance is documenting all the work performed for each system. Keeping a history of what was done and what the current symptoms are will help with this problem and with future diagnostics.

A maintenance log includes:

- Date and time

- Technician's name

- The computer name

List the other items that would be useful on a maintenance log:

_____
_____
_____
_____
_____
_____
_____
_____
_____
_____

Troubleshooting Tools and Aids

Every technician should have a good tool set. To correctly troubleshoot hardware problems, technicians need to be equipped with the right tools. The average computer problem is not going to require sophisticated tools. Usually a screwdriver and a nut driver are all that is required. However, technicians should be prepared for a wide range of circumstances. The tools in a good tool set include both mechanical and digital tools. Technicians should plan ahead if they are going to work away from their tech-bench and to bring the necessary tools. The typical tool set includes items such as:

- Flat-head screwdriver

- Phillips-head screwdriver

- Nut drivers

- Needle-nose pliers

- Diagonals or cross-cut pliers

- Mirror – helps see into very tight spots

- Digital multimeter

- Flashlight

What is a digital multimeter (DMM)?

_____
_____
_____
_____
_____
_____
_____
_____

Vocabulary Terms

Define the following:

Voltage (V): _____
_____
_____

Current (Amps or A): _____
_____
_____

Watts (W): _____
_____
_____

Resistance (Ohms or R): _____
_____
_____

Capacitors: _____
_____
_____

DC voltage test: _____
_____
_____

Resistance or continuity test:_____
_____
_____

AC voltage test: _____
_____
_____

Loop back plugs: _____
_____
_____

A normal vacuum should never be used on computer components. Why? _____
_____
_____
_____

Environment Guidelines

As with other computing devices, a computer eventually comes to an end-of-life. List three of the reasons this happens:

_____
_____
_____
_____

Eventually, the question arises: What to do with the old computers or parts? Can they simply be placed in the garbage bin so that they are hauled to the landfill and buried?

Computers and peripherals contain some environmentally unfriendly materials. Most computer components are either hazardous or contain some level of hazardous substances. Waste materials are listed as hazardous because they are known to be harmful to human health and the environment when not managed properly. Also known as toxic waste, hazardous materials typically contain high concentrations of heavy metals, such as cadmium, lead, or mercury. Computer printed circuit boards consist of plastics, precious metals, fiberglass, arsenic, silicon, gallium, and lead. CRTs (monitors) contain glass, metal, plastics, lead, barium, and rare earth metals. Batteries from portable systems can contain lead, cadmium, lithium, alkaline manganese, and mercury.

Material Safety Data Sheet (MSDS)

To determine if a material used in PC repairs or preventive maintenance is classified as hazardous, consult the MSDS. In addition to the solvents and chemicals already identified, the Occupational Safety and Health Administration (OSHA) has developed a series of data sheets on hazardous materials indicating hazards and their handling. All hazardous materials are required to have a MSDS accompany them when they change hands. This means that some of the products purchased for computer repairs or maintenance come with relevant MSDS information in the manual.

What information is included on a MSDS?

_____
_____
_____
_____
_____
_____
_____
_____
_____
_____

OSHA requires that a MSDS be posted prominently in organizations that work directly with these materials.

How can you safely dispose of computer components and conserve natural resources?

_____
_____

Batteries

Batteries often contain rare earth metals that can be harmful to the environment. Typically batteries from portable computer systems can contain lead, cadmium, lithium, alkaline manganese, and mercury.

Why are these metals so harmful to the environment?

_____
_____
_____

Mercury, being one of the elements commonly used in the manufacture of batteries, is extremely toxic (harmful) to humans. Lead and the other metals, although not as harmful as mercury, can still cause problems to the environment.

How are depleted batteries classified? _____

If possible, what is the preferred method to dispose of batteries? _____

CRTs

The safety concerns that are directly related to the computer monitor, otherwise called the cathode ray tube (CRT), cannot be over emphasized. One way to appreciate the potential hazard associated with monitors is to understand how they work.

Monitors work by directing electrons at the screen under the guide of a powerful magnet.

What are electrons? _____

When electrons hit the front of the screen, they are really striking a coating that is applied to the inside of the monitor. The coating is known as phosphor.

What is phosphor?

_____
_____
_____
_____
_____

CRTs that have come to an end-of-life must always be handled with care because of a potentially lethal voltage that is maintained even after being disconnected from power. Additionally, CRTs contain glass, metal, plastics, lead, barium, and rare earth metals. According to the Environmental Protection Agency (EPA), CRT monitors contain four pounds of lead on average (the exact amount depends on size and make). Lead and many of the other metals have been cited as toxic; therefore, they are harmful to the environment and humans.

If possible, what is the preferred method to dispose of CRTs? _____

Toner Kits, Cartridges, and Developers

Used toner kits, cartridges, and developers can be destructive to the environment, and their sheer volume necessitates caution in the way that they are handled and disposed.

There are a couple of ways to deal with laser and inkjet printer cartridges. List them:

_____
_____

Chemical Solvents and Aerosol Cans

The chemicals and solvents that clean computers are another source of environmental problems. When leached (drained or evaporated) into the environment, these chemicals can cause significant damage.

When it comes to the chemical solvents that clean computers, and the containers they come in, it is normally necessary to clear these items with the local waste management agencies before disposing of them. As with batteries, contact your sanitation provider to find out how and where to dispose of these chemicals.

Never dump them down the sink or dispose of them in any drain that connects to the public sewers (the underground pipeline that collects municipal liquid waste from households or industry).

What are free liquids? _____
_____
_____
_____

If not disposed of properly, what can happen to aerosol cans that are not completely used up? _____

How can you safely dispose of computer components and conserve natural resources?
_____
_____

Electrostatic Discharge (ESD)

Ever gotten a zap from a doorknob in a carpeted room? If so, then you know static electricity. Static electricity is the buildup of an electric charge resting on a surface. If there is a buildup of static electricity, it can end up zapping a computer component and causing irreversible damage.

A zap is formally known as ESD. ESD is the worst enemy of the fine electronics found in computer systems.

How many volts must be built up for a person to get a zap? _____

How many volts must be built up to cause damage to a computer? _

How many volts must be built up to feel pain or hear the zap? _____

What is a wrist strap? _____
_____

When should a wrist strap be worn? _____
_____

When should a wrist strap not be worn? _____

_____

An ESD free environment is crucial to preventive maintenance that involves opening the computer case. List some key elements to an ESD free environment:

_____
_____
_____
_____
_____
_____

Computer Preventive Maintenance

There are many things that can cause a computer system to fail physically. The most common are dust buildup, extreme temperatures, and rough handling. Describe the best way to handle the following maintenance tasks:

Dust inside the computer case: _____
_____
_____
_____

Fingerprints on the CRT or LCD screen: _____
_____
_____
_____

Dirt build-up inside the mouse: _____
_____
_____
_____

Dirt and dust in the keyboard: _____
_____
_____
_____

Glass on the scanner is smudged: _____
_____
_____
_____

All printers have moving parts and require a higher level of maintenance. Printers produce impurities that collect on the components within the device. Over time, these impurities need to be cleaned out; otherwise, they can cause the printer to malfunction.

Describe the best way to maintain the following:

Dot-matrix printer: _____
_____
_____

Inkjet printer: _____
_____
_____

Laser printer: _____
_____
_____

Why is it important to choose the right type of paper for a printer? _____
_____
_____

Environmental Guidelines for a Server Room

In the server room, temperature is important. Never put the server against ductwork or next to the air conditioner. Be aware of items that can cause interference with electrical pull (motors, microwaves, and the like) and electromagnetic interference (EMI) , and try to use only isolated grounding circuits.

The area around the server should be kept free of debris and clutter. Ideally, the server should be locked in a closet with limited access and no likelihood of being bumped, jostled, accessed directly, or otherwise disturbed by non-administrators.

What is plenum? _____
_____
_____

Why is humidity a factor in a server room? _____
_____
_____

What type of fire suppression is preferable in a server room? _____
_____

What type of fire suppression is the worst for a server room? _____
_____

Discuss the steps to take in the event of an impending flood: _____

_____

_____

_____

_____

_____

Why is a disaster recovery plan crucial in a network environment? _____

_____

_____

_____

_____

_____

Preventive Maintenance Software

Several utilities that are included with DOS and Windows that help maintain system integrity are listed below. If run on a regular basis, these utilities can make the system run faster and more efficiently. Describe the following utilities:

Scandisk: _____

_____

_____

Defrag: _____

_____

_____

CHKDSK /f: _____

_____

_____

REGEDIT: _____

_____

_____

Anti-Virus

Computer viruses are programs that have been written by people with malicious intent. After a virus has been released, it can do anything from take control of a computer and leave a message on the screen or completely erase your hard drive. After a computer has been infected, the virus can be spread to other machines either by way of a network connection or by removable media.

To prevent a virus from infecting the system, the best defense is an anti-virus application. Anti-virus programs, after they are installed, can run in the background to make sure a virus is not infecting the computer. They can also be run on command and scan your entire computer or just a specific file for viruses. If a virus is found, the anti-virus software can perform one of two actions:

- It can clean the infected file, or

- If it can't clean the file, it can isolate the file.

If a file becomes isolated, or quarantined, the user will not be able to open it.

How often should anti-virus software be updated? _____

List the most common forms of viruses and how they infect a computer system:

_____
_____
_____

_____
_____
_____

_____
_____
_____

Power Vocabulary

Define the following terms relating to power issues:

Blackouts: _____
_____
_____

Brownouts: _____
_____
_____

Noise: _____
_____
_____

Spikes: _____
_____
_____

Surges: _____
_____
_____

Surge suppressor: _____
_____
_____

Standby Power Supply: _____
_____
_____

Uninterruptible Power Supply: _____
_____
_____

Overall, the best solution for power events is having a properly grounded building and enough battery power to run all equipment in case of a power outage.

Concept Question

Many preventive maintenance tasks can be automated although many must be done manually. Describe the routines that can be set to run on a regular basis and what items cannot.

_____
_____
_____
_____
_____
_____
_____
_____
_____
_____
_____
_____
_____
_____
_____
_____
_____

Additional Notes

_____
_____
_____
_____
_____
_____
_____
_____
_____
_____
_____
_____
_____
_____
_____
_____
_____
_____
_____
_____

Labs and Worksheets

The following labs and worksheets are available in the CISCO NETWORKING ACADEMY PROGRAM IT Essentials I: PC Hardware and Software Lab Companion and as part of the online curriculum. Labs and worksheets are an excellent tool that you can use to help reinforce the material covered in this chapter.

Labs

11.1.2   Using a Digital Multimeter (PDF, 14 KB)
11.3.6   Cleaning Computer Components
11.4.1   Using the Scandisk and Defrag Utilities (PDF, 9 KB)

Worksheets

11.1.3   Environmental Considerations (PDF, 6 KB)
11.2.1   Electrostatic Discharge (ESD) (PDF, 6 KB)
11.5.2   Preventive Maintenance for Components

A+ Exam Review Questions

The following are review questions for the A+ exam. Answers are found in Appendix A.

1.   A technician's tool set should include all of the following except?
   a.   Lint-free cloths

   b.   Canned air

   c.   Regular vacuum

   d.   Various solvents

2.   The most desired method of disposing of computer components?
   a.   Recycling

   b.   Trash can

   c.   Call the Chamber of Commerce

   d.   Have them crushed to save space

3.   What are MSDS?
   a.   Material Specifications Distribution Sheets

   b.   Monitor Safety Data Sheets

   c.   Material Safety and Data Sheets

   d.   Monitor Specifications Detail Sheets

4.   How do you properly dispose of computer equipment?
   a.   Take the equipment to a landfill instead of using a trash can

   b.   Call a proper waste disposal site for pickup or deliver to an appropriate disposal site

   c.   Remove the serial numbers before disposing of the equipment

   d.   Donate the equipment to a non-profit group that can dispose of it

5.   High voltage equipment can cause?
   a.   Burns

   b.   Blindness

   c.   Headaches

   d.   Cancer

6. How many volts can a standard CRT in a monitor hold?
   a. Up to 25,000
   b. Up to 3000
   c. Up to 6000
   d. Up to 60,000

7. What is a zap?
   a. A safety device
   b. A computer chip resistant to ESD
   c. ESD
   d. A CRT

8. What are BTUs in relation to the server?
   a. Bright Thermometer Units
   b. British Thermal Units
   c. British Temperature Uploads
   d. British Target Units

9. What type of material can prevent the build-up of static electricity in carpet?
   a. Rubber
   b. Rayon
   c. Nylon
   d. Plastic

10. Cabling designed to be used without conduit in plenums, walls, and other areas is?
    a. Twisted-pair cable
    b. Coaxial cable
    c. PVC cable
    d. Plenum-grade coaxial cable

11. How do you remove the dust from inside the computer?
    a. A small vacuum
    b. Blow out the dust using your lungs
    c. Wipe gently with a damp cloth
    d. Use non-static compressed air

12. What is the optimal temperature for a server room?
    a. 50 – 95 degrees
    b. 35 degrees
    c. 100 degrees
    d. 40 – 50 degrees

13. The best way to store circuit boards is?
    a. In a cool, dry place
    b. Between sheets of Styrofoam
    c. In anti-static bags
    d. In a cool, humid place

14. One way to protect computer equipment from lightning is to?
    a. Ground the equipment using a lightning rod on the roof
    b. Use overhand loose knots in the power cord
    c. Use a power strip for the monitor
    d. Use an uninterruptible power supply for the air conditioning

15. A brownout is?
    a. A slightly elevated voltage that lasts for seconds or minutes or more
    b. A slightly decreased voltage that lasts for seconds or minutes or more
    c. A power failure that lasts for seconds or minutes or more
    d. Alternating power out, power on that lasts for seconds or minutes or more

16. A sudden increase in voltage that is much higher than other levels is?
    a. Spike
    b. Noise
    c. Surge
    d. Power

17. What does UPS stand for?
    a. Universal Power Services
    b. Uninterruptible Power Source
    c. Uninterruptible Power Supply
    d. Universal Power Supply

18.   What checks the integrity of files and folders?

    a.   Scandisk

    b.   Defrag

    c.   Regedit

    d.   Checkerdisk

19.   The most common type of virus that modifies existing programs?

    a.   Macro virus

    b.   CPU virus

    c.   File virus

    d.   E-mail virus

20.   The best preventive maintenance advice is to?

    a.   Make backups of important files regularly

    b.   Keep the system clean and away from dust

    c.   Use system utility software

    d.   All of the above

Chapter 12

Troubleshooting Hardware

This chapter focuses on the problems that affect hardware in a computer system. Effective troubleshooting uses techniques to diagnose and fix computer problems. A series of logical steps speeds up the troubleshooting process. Rarely will simply guessing potential solutions for a problem work. It is best to use the troubleshooting steps.

Troubleshooting Steps

Troubleshooting is a cycle. There are six steps in the troubleshooting cycle. These steps are important to successfully determine the cause and solution for a problem.

List and explain each of the troubleshooting steps:

1. _____
_____
_____
_____
_____
_____
_____
_____

2. _____
_____
_____
_____
_____
_____
_____
_____

3. _____
_____
_____
_____
_____
_____
_____

4. _____

_____

_____

_____

_____

_____

_____

5. _____

_____

_____

_____

_____

_____

_____

6. _____

_____

_____

_____

_____

_____

_____

Why is documenting considered the most important step?_____

_____

_____

_____

There are specific questions regarding the network server that a technician should ask in the event of a problem. List four of these questions:

1. _____

_____

_____

_____

_____

2._____

_____

_____

_____

_____

3.

_____

_____

_____

_____

_____

4.

_____

_____

_____

_____

_____

A good troubleshooter uses his or her senses to help find problems. List the senses you would use and what they can tell you about the system:

_____

_____

_____

_____

_____

_____

_____

_____

_____

Field Replaceable Units

A device that can be replaced or added in the field is called a field replaceable unit (FRU). FRUs do not require any soldering and are easy to remove and install. A sound card, for example, can be removed with no special tools required. List other common FRUs:

_____

_____

_____

_____

_____

_____

_____

POST Errors

Every time the computer is turned on, it runs through a power-on self test (POST). The POST is a series of self-diagnostic tests that the computer runs through to test the major hardware. It is the first task run by the computer's Basic Input/Output System (BIOS). The POST performs basic test routines on the motherboard and major hardware devices. It does not perform in-depth testing on the computer system. It can only detect major failures that will prohibit the boot-up process.

Where is POST stored in the computer? _____
_____

What is a POST card? _____
_____

CMOS/BIOS Errors

The BIOS is a good place to start diagnosing hardware problems. The features of BIOS provide technicians with low-level hardware and software configuration information. Although the BIOS provides low-level information, it is extremely useful when troubleshooting computer hardware.

List the solutions to the following errors:

CMOS checksum errors: _____
_____
_____

Incorrect CPU speed: _____
_____
_____

Inaccessible boot device:_____
_____
_____

Incorrect memory size: _____
_____
_____

Identifying the faulty/incorrect CMOS setting: _____
_____
_____

A BIOS upgrade can include patches, fixes, additional features, and additional support for the latest devices that should resolve any problems. However, it is not recommended to upgrade the BIOS if problems do not exist. If the system is operational, BIOS upgrades are risky and should be avoided. If the BIOS is updated incorrectly, it could damage the motherboard and peripheral devices.

What special considerations should be taken before upgrading the BIOS?

_____

_____

_____

_____

_____

_____

_____

_____

Motherboard-Related Errors

The motherboard coordinates the proper functioning of the system components. It allows devices to communicate and work in harmony with each other. Troubleshooting a dead computer system is a process of elimination. The technician will start from the outside and work down to the motherboard. What is the typical fix for a malfunctioning motherboard?

_____

_____

_____

The computer will not boot and appears"dead. What is the first device to check?_____

_____

CPU

Symptoms of a processor error can include slow performance, POST beep errors, or a system that is not operating properly. These errors usually indicate that an internal error has occurred. Internal errors might also cause failures to be intermittent. The CPU might begin a task, then fail. If the system continuously counts RAM or freezes while counting the RAM, the CPU is creating the errors and might need to be replaced.

Requirements for a CPU to work with a motherboard include voltage, socket type, and clock speeds.

Troubleshooting the CPU involves two issues. List them below:

1. _____

2._____

RAM

Today, most random-access memory (RAM) implementations are SDRAM and RDRAM. SDRAM with 168-pin DIMM are the most common modules. Before SDRAM and RDRAM, there was DRAM. Older Pentiums used FPM and EDO RAM. FPM and EDO RAM are 72-pin memory modules.

RAM failures come in two forms: sudden or intermittent. Overused or bad memory can cause the system to fail at anytime. What would indicate bad memory to a technician?

_____
_____
_____
_____
_____
_____
_____

What should be considered when installing or purchasing RAM modules? _____
_____
_____

Cable Issues

Many cabling issues are usually because of faulty physical connections and reconnecting cables can resolve many problems. What are other cabling issues to consider when troubleshooting?

_____
_____
_____
_____
_____
_____

Ports

Port problems are typically diagnosed with a slow performing or inoperative peripheral device. Common symptoms include the following:

- Completely inoperative port

- Device not found error error message

- Peripheral device is slow, or performance is bad

List the issues that can be attributed to a problem with a port:

_____
_____
_____
_____
_____
_____

Video System

Typically, when a computer is having video display errors, the system will boot normally but there will be no video display. If these circumstances exist, the technician is probably accurate in assuming that the error is with the video display.

Where should the troubleshooting begin? _____

Because of the potentially fatal voltage in a computer monitor, it should never be opened except by a technician certified to repair high voltage components.

Explain how to troubleshoot a system with two video cards:

_____
_____
_____
_____

Hard Drives

Some computers are configured with two hard drives. This increases space for backups and storing data. Explain the master/slave relationship:

_____
_____
_____
_____

Describe what causes the majority of problems with hard drives:

_____
_____
_____
_____

Sound Cards

Today, most sound cards are Plug and Play (PnP).

Explain the first troubleshooting steps for sound problems:

_____
_____
_____
_____
_____
_____
_____
_____

Intermittent problems or a dead sound card usually indicates symptoms of resource conflicts. If the sound card is in conflict with another device, it might operate sporadically. For example, if the sound card does not work when a document is printed, this might indicate that resources are conflicting. They might have been configured to use the same interrupt request line (IRQ) channel.

Describe the steps in troubleshooting sound card conflict problems?

_____
_____
_____
_____
_____

Sometimes, sound card problems are caused by conflicts. Where would you go to check on device conflicts?

_____

Power Supply Issues

The power supply plays a vital role in the operation of any computer system. If the power supply is not working properly, the computer components will be receiving the wrong voltages and will not operate correctly. The power supply is attached to numerous devices that rely on it for power. The power supply converts the current coming from the wall jack from alternating current (AC) into direct current (DC). The AC coming from the wall is 120 or 240 V (depending on the country or region) and is converted into DC +/-5 and +/-12 V. After the current is converted from AC to DC, the power supply provides two important functions to the computer. List them:

1. _____
_____
_____
_____

2. _____
_____
_____
_____

Cooling Issues

Computer components are susceptible to heat. The components operate at high speeds and in tight spaces. For example, hard drives operate at 7200 rpm and can be located centimeters from one another. This environment is conducive to heat build-up, which is an enemy to the components. Every computer case needs proper airflow for the components to perform at their optimal levels. The design of the computer case should maximize airflow.

What generates the majority of airflow? _____

What do onboard fans do? _____

How do you verify that the fans are working? _____

Why would additional fans be added to a system? _____
_____
_____

Troubleshooting Input Devices

When troubleshooting input devices, always start with the simple solutions. Check to make sure that the device is properly connected. Verify that the cable is in good working condition and is not frayed. As with any hardware problem, start from the outside of the box.

After checking the physical connections of the input device, try rebooting the computer. Sometimes, an input device will be disconnected while in operation and a reboot is required. Pay attention to any errors that display during startup. The errors will be indicated either as a text error on the video display or a POST beep code. For example, if a keyboard is not properly connected, the user might get a beep code or a 301 error message.

Two common errors with input devices are incorrect character input and unrecognized devices. Both of these errors can result from a bad or outdated driver. Always check the manufacturer's web site for updated device drivers. Input devices will need the right driver to work correctly.

The tables that follow list various problems/errors. Provide a solution for each problem/error listed in the space provided within the table:

Problem/ Error	Solution
Keyboard is running on legacy equipment and isn't supported	
Gate A20 failure	
Voltage issue	
Keyboard isn't properly connected (301 error message or keyboard error)	

Problem/ Error	Solution
Common Mouse Problems	
Unrecognized or malfunctioning mouse	
Erratic movement of the cursor	
Common Scanner Problems	
Bad software installation; device isn't recognized	
Quality of image is low on monitor	
Slow or bad performance	
Vertical streak on image	
Common Parallel Port Errors	
Cable can't supply the necessary data transfer rates	
Legacy equipment doesn't support new product requirements or there is a hardware defect	
Outdated or bad drivers	
IRQ conflict; two devices sharing same device	
Wrong mode selected (EPP, ECP, or EPP/ECP modes)	

USB Ports

What does USB stand for? _____

Most new computers will be equipped with a Universal Serial Bus (USB) port. Today, USB ports are replacing the older serial port found on most computers. USB devices are based upon PnP technology. This means that USB devices should install and operate with minimal configuration. However, this does not mean that USB devices are free from errors.

The most common failures with USB devices are:

1. _____

2. _____

3. _____

4. _____

USB devices connect through USB cables. They come in two speeds: low and high. Why should the device and cable be at the same speed? _____
_____
_____
_____

Troubleshooting Printers

The printer communicates with the computer when the user has a request for a document (output). Printers are heavily used and problems can arise because of this constant wear and tear. It is essential that end users and technicians perform preventative maintenance on the printer. Preventive maintenance will help alleviate problems before there is a critical failure. Proper cleaning of the printer can reduce downtime, loss of productivity, and repair cost.

What are the most common printer problems:

_____
_____
_____
_____
_____
_____
_____
_____

SCSI Interface Issues

Small Computer System Interface (SCSI) drives require a separate controller from the Integrated Drive Electronics (IDE) controller. This controller operates with read-only memory (ROM) BIOS under Disk Operating System (DOS) and Windows. The ROM BIOS contains management, surface verification, and low-level format applications. SCSI BIOS is accessed during the boot up process by pressing the setup key combination.

What are the SCSI bus operation and the transfer rate controlled by?

_____

Why should SCSI devices have unique SCSI IDs? _____
_____
_____
_____
_____
_____

What are I/O errors? _____
_____
_____
_____
_____
_____

What are fixed disk I/O errors? _____
_____
_____
_____
_____
_____

What is a SCSI termination point? _____
_____
_____
_____

Internet/Network Access Devices

Troubleshooting network problems range from an unattached CAT 5 cable to advanced protocol issues. Discussing advanced network problems is beyond the scope of this chapter.

Begin network troubleshooting by determining if there has been any recent change to the system. If there has been a change to the system, it might be causing the problem. Reverse the changes and see if the problem is resolved.

Explain the basic steps for troubleshooting the following for:

Cabling: _____
_____
_____
_____
_____
_____

NIC and Modem: _____
_____
_____
_____
_____
_____

Concept Question

A user has reported that their computer has been locking up. You have no other information. Explain the steps to troubleshoot the problem.

_____
_____
_____
_____
_____
_____
_____
_____
_____
_____
_____
_____
_____
_____
_____
_____
_____
_____
_____

Additional Notes

_____
_____
_____
_____
_____
_____
_____
_____
_____
_____
_____
_____
_____
_____
_____
_____
_____
_____

Labs and Worksheets

The following labs and worksheets are available in the *Cisco Networking Academy Program IT Essentials I: PC Hardware and Software Lab Companion* and as part of the online curriculum. Labs and worksheets are an excellent tool that you can use to help reinforce the material covered in this chapter.

Labs

12.1.7 The Steps of the Troubleshooting Cycle
12.2.3 Identifying POST Errors

Worksheets

12.1.2 Troubleshooting Basics
12.3.2 Troubleshooting Printers
12.3.4 Troubleshooting Hardware

A+ Exam Review Questions

The following are review questions for the A+ exam. Answers are found in Appendix A.

1.   What is the first step in troubleshooting a PC problem?
   a.   Remove the cover
   b.   Unplug all the cords from the computer
   c.   Remove all optional equipment from the system
   d.   Eliminate the user as the source

2.   What setting should the multimeter be set to when checking a power supply unit?
   a.   AC voltage
   b.   DC voltage
   c.   Ohms
   d.   Amps

3.   How many changes should you make at a time when troubleshooting a PC?
   a.   One
   b.   Two
   c.   Three
   d.   It doesn't matter

4.   What is the most likely cause for a shaky video display?
   a.   Faulty monitor
   b.   Faulty cables
   c.   Faulty video adapter
   d.   Incorrect settings

5.   The first thing to do if a new monitor is not working is?
   a.   Adjust the brightness and contrast
   b.   Check the monitor for broken parts
   c.   Measure the voltage inside the monitor
   d.   Make sure the power cord is firmly plugged in

6.   What would cause a monitor to fade?
   a.   Electron guns clog up with electrons
   b.   Phosphor coatings wear away
   c.   Brightness controls fail over time
   d.   Fluorescent tubing interferes with monitors

7.   According to the AMI BIOS post errors, a beep code with one long beep and two short beeps during the boot up indicates that there is a problem with?
   a.   Video system
   b.   Floppy drive
   c.   Hard drive
   d.   Mouse

8.   If a power supply fan is running and the hard drive spins up but the system seems dead, what might be the problem?
   a.   The monitor is turned off
   b.   A faulty expansion card has disabled the system
   c.   The hard drive is bad
   d.   The system board is bad

9.   What is the problem if after five minutes the computer continually locks up?
   a.   Broken power supply
   b.   There is a DMA conflict
   c.   Faulty keyboard
   d.   The CPU fan might not be working

10.   What is the problem if the time resets when you turn the computer off?
   a.   A bad CMOS battery
   b.   A bad BIOS chip
   c.   Faulty power cord
   d.   Faulty motherboard

11.   A new mouse has been installed but does not work, what is the problem?
   a.   It is plugged into the wrong port
   b.   It requires a new driver
   c.   The operating system needs to be re-installed
   d.   It is a faulty mouse

12. A jumpy mouse is most likely because of?
   a. One of the potentiometers has failed
   b. Corrupt mouse driver
   c. The mouse is plugged into the wrong port
   d. The mouse needs cleaning

13. What will create a memory problem?
   a. Installing different speed memory modules
   b. Skipping over an empty memory socket
   c. Not installing memory in pairs
   d. Using memory from different manufacturers

14. One of your memory modules is hot. What does this indicate?
   a. It is normal
   b. It needs a new cooling fan
   c. The voltage to the memory is insufficient
   d. It is dead or dying

15. What symbol is typically used in Windows to indicate a disabled hardware device?
   a. A red X through the device name
   b. A circled exclamation point on the hardware icon
   c. An upside down question mark
   d. A blinking, red X

16. What symbol is typically used in Windows to indicate a hardware conflict?
   a. A question mark on the hardware icon
   b. A circled exclamation point on the hardware icon
   c. An upside down question mark
   d. A blinking, red X

17. A management tool for RAM is?
   a. POST
   b. MEM.EXE
   c. MEMMAKER.EXE
   d. HIMEM.SYS

18. The computer fails to start after installing a new sound card. What is the most likely cause of this problem?

    a.   The sound card is not compatible

    b.   There is not enough memory present in the system

    c.   Interrupt conflict between the sound card and another device

    d.   The sound card needs a different DMA setting

19. A computer powers up but won't attach to the network. A possible solution is?

    a.   Reconfigure the NIC

    b.   Check Device Manager for network adapter conflicts

    c.   Restart the computer

    d.   Perform diagnostic tests on the server

20. The best source for troubleshooting information is?

    a.   The user

    b.   The manufacturer's web site

    c.   Other technicians

    d.   All of the above

Chapter 13

Troubleshooting Software

This chapter focuses on troubleshooting software that diagnoses and fixes system problems. The troubleshooting process should begin with the end user because they have the most valuable information. Their input will help narrow the search for the problem that is affecting the computer. Whether or not the end user is a direct result of the problem, the main goal of troubleshooting is to get the end user working with their system. The two important things to do to determine what type of error has occurred are the following:

- Reproduce the error

- Identify changes to the system

After determining what the problem is and where the problem exists, it is time to fix the software. Fixing the software depends on what the problem was that prevented it from working. It might be necessary to copy some files from the installation CD of the operating system or a CD of an application that was installed back to the hard drive.

It might be necessary to change some paths of the shortcuts to point to the executable of the application that was installed. Sometimes just reinstalling the software will repair anything that was damaged. It all depends on the cause of the software errors.

System Boot Problems

The boot up procedure that starts the computer system reveals a lot about the health of the system. Observing the steps of a boot up process can reveal a great deal about what is causing problems in the system. The possible cause of errors can be eliminated or determined during the boot up procedure. If the problem lies in the boot up process then only some of those steps will be observed.

Knowing the details of each step of the boot process will help determine what section failed if the system will not boot up past that step. For example, if the system boots up all the way to the point where it is checking the floppy drive, and the floppy drive light does not come on, the problem exists in the floppy drive.

Explain the following:

Bootable disk: _____
_____
_____
_____

Hidden files: _____

_____

_____

_____

Command interpreter: _____

_____

_____

_____

DOS switches: _____

_____

_____

_____

Bootable disk utility files: _____

_____

_____

_____

Format.exe: _____

_____

_____

_____

FDISK.EXE/MBR: _____

_____

_____

_____

Bootable configuration files: _____

_____

_____

_____

DOS Error Messages

Error messages are another common operating system troubleshooting issue. Many things can cause these error messages to display. As a technician's experience with troubleshooting computer systems increases, these messages become easier to recognize. Technicians will eventually learn their causes and how to address them. Error messages usually pop up when the operating system identifies a problem or when an end user attempts to run an application that the operating system cannot recognize.

Explain what the following error messages indicate:

Bad or Missing COMMAND.COM: _____
_____
_____
_____

Configuration File Errors: _____
_____
_____
_____

REM statements: _____
_____
_____
_____

Extended Memory Access (HIMEM.SYS): _____
_____
_____
_____

Expanded Memory Access (EMM386.EXE): _____
_____
_____
_____

LASTDRIVE = Errors: _____
_____
_____
_____

DEVICEHIGH = Errors: _____
_____
_____
_____

What are Invalid Directory errors?

_____
_____
_____
_____

Troubleshooting Windows

Most of the setup problems are errors that occur during the installation phase of the operating system. The early versions of the Disk Operating System (DOS) required simple installations. However, with the latest versions of Windows, the setup procedures have become a complex issue that requires running an install or setup program. Therefore, technicians will spend more time than ever before on troubleshooting Setup problems.

One of the most common types of installation problems occurs while attempting to install the operating system on the hard drive.

The error message, *The system's hard drive does not have enough space to carry out the installation process* has displayed. What should be done to perform the installation?

_____
_____
_____
_____

If the system produces an error message or a beep-coded error signal before the beep signaling that the Basic Input/Output System (BIOS) has passed successfully and the operating system is about to load, the problem is most likely hardware related.

If the error message or beep-coded error message occurs after the beep signaling that the BIOS has passed successfully and the operating system is about to load, the problem is most likely in the operating system or is software related.

Why is a system startup disk important to have?

_____
_____
_____
_____

The Windows operating system provides many other troubleshooting tools. These tools are referred to as System Troubleshooting tools. They can be used to isolate and correct issues and can be helpful when troubleshooting a system.

What is MSCONFIG.EXE used for?

_____
_____
_____
_____

Memory usage errors occur when the operating system or an application attempts to access a memory location that is unallocated. When this type of conflict occurs, the unallocated memory location becomes corrupted and usually results in the operating system crashing. This could occur if a user is running more than one application at a time and one of the applications attempts to use another application's memory space. When this happens, the operating system will generate an error message or just stop processing altogether and lock up. This typical error message is *This operation has performed an illegal operation and is about to be shut down.*

What happens when the Windows Resource Levels get too low?

_____
_____
_____
_____

What is a GPF?

_____
_____
_____
_____

What is a VxD file?

_____
_____
_____
_____

What is a DLL?

_____
_____
_____
_____

A command line utility that scans the OS files to ensure that they are correct is called:

_____

What does pressing the **Ctrl+Alt+Del** buttons accomplish?

_____
_____

What should be done prior to upgrading to a Windows 9x OS?

_____

_____

_____

_____

Describe the best way to troubleshoot the following:

No Operating System Found: _____

_____

_____

_____

Windows Protection Error: _____

_____

_____

_____

Illegal Operation: _____

_____

_____

_____

Device Not Found: _____

_____

_____

_____

What is Safe Mode used for? _____

_____

_____

_____

What are the benefits of troubleshooting in DOS mode? _____

_____

_____

_____

_____

Windows 9x maintains error log files of system operations that show which events happened before the error. The filenames indicate the type of information tracked.

List the four common log files and what they are used for:

1. _____

_____

_____

2. _____
   _____
   _____
   _____

3. _____
   _____
   _____
   _____

4. _____
   _____
   _____
   _____

Virtual Memory Errors

Virtual memory is really just part of the hard drive that is reserved for the operating system to do what is called paging. Data is stored in memory in pages, and only a certain number of these can fit in physical memory (random-access memory [RAM]) at any given time. Therefore, the operating system takes some of these pages and moves them out to virtual memory, so that the more current pages (usually the ones for the program being used at the moment) can be kept in physical memory, which is faster.

This process is often referred to as swapping, hence the term swap file. The swap file is essentially one huge file that contains often thousands of these pages on a reserved portion of the hard drive.

Explain virtual memory settings:

_____
_____
_____
_____
_____
_____
_____

List the common causes of swap file errors:

_____
_____
_____
_____
_____
_____
_____
_____

System Tools

Both Windows 9x and 2000 have many system tools that are helpful when troubleshooting. They can provide a number of administrative and diagnostic tools to help fix problems with the computer system.

Explain the following:

Event Viewer: _____
_____
_____
_____

Dr. Watson TSR Utility: _____
_____
_____
_____

DEFRAG.EXE: _____
_____
_____
_____

CHKDSK.EXE: _____
_____
_____
_____

SCANDSKW.EXE: _____
_____
_____
_____

MSCONFIG.EXE: _____
_____
_____
_____

The Windows Device Manager provides a way to view the hardware on the system in a graphical interface while also helping to manage and troubleshoot it. Device Manager disables, un-installs, and updates device drivers. Device Manager helps to determine whether the hardware on the computer is working properly and if the correct drivers are installed for the hardware.

What symbols indicate problems in the Device Manager? _____
_____
_____

Using the Device Manager, how do you update drivers? _____

_____

_____

_____

_____

Windows System Editors

Windows System Editors allow settings to be changed and customized to whatever policy the system administrator requires. A system administrator can use the SYSEDIT.EXE and POLEDIT.EXE editor to edit configuration settings to the user interface. In Windows 2000, the Group Policy Editor (GPE) allows the administrator to edit a policy for an entire group of users at one time.

Explain the following system editors:

SYSEDIT.EXE: _____

_____

_____

_____

POLEDIT.EXE: _____

_____

_____

_____

Group Policy Editor: _____

_____

_____

_____

Registry Files

The Registry files contain all the system configuration information. This includes the local hardware configuration, the network environment, file associations, and user configurations. User.dat and System.dat are the Registry files that contain all of the contents in the Registry.

Explain the following Registry files:

USER.DAT: _____

_____

_____

USER.DA0: _____
_____
_____

SYSTEM.DAT: _____
_____
_____

SYSTEM.DA0: _____
_____
_____

SYSTEM.INI: _____
_____
_____

WIN.INI: _____
_____
_____

The Registry Structure

It is important to understand the Registry subtrees to effectively troubleshoot and maintain the computer. Every process that is running on the system has a key.

Explain the following subtree keys:

HKEY_USERS: _____
_____
_____

HKEY_CURRENT_CONFIG: _____
_____
_____

HKEY_CLASSES_ROOT: _____
_____
_____

HKEY_CURRENT_USER: _____
_____
_____

HKEY_LOCAL_MACHINE: _____
_____
_____

How do you access the Registry? _____
_____
_____

What are the benefits of third party registry editing tools? _____
_____
_____

Windows Recovery Console

The Windows 2000 Recovery Console is a command-line interface that performs a variety of troubleshooting and recovery tasks. These include starting and stopping services, reading and writing data on a local drive (including drives that are formatted with the NTFS file system), and formatting hard disks. After the recovery console has been started, use the commands from the command line to remove, replace, or copy corrupt files.

Explain the two ways to access the recovery console:

_____
_____

What is FIXMBR? _____
_____
_____

Data Backup and Recovery

By performing regular backups and with recovery tools, the technician can prevent data loss and reinstall the operating system if necessary. The method for backing up the Registry depends on the operating system.

What is the blue screen of death? _____
_____
_____

Describe the following backup methods and explain the advantages and disadvantages of each:

Normal backup: _____
_____
_____

Advantages: _____
_____
_____

Disadvantages: _____
_____
_____

Incremental backup: _____
_____
_____

Advantages: _____
_____
_____

Disadvantages: _____
_____
_____

Differential backup: _____
_____
_____

Advantages: _____
_____
_____

Disadvantages: _____
_____
_____

Windows Networking Software Connection Troubleshooting

Problems with computer networks can be challenging. Having a thorough understanding of the network setup provides a starting point when troubleshooting.

What should be done when presented with the following?

Cannot log onto Network – NIC not functioning: _____
_____
_____

Incorrect Parameter Setting/Switches:_____
_____
_____

Incorrect Protocols/Properties: _____
_____
_____

Incorrect Client/Client Properties: _____
_____
_____

Missing or Incorrect Bindings: _____
_____
_____

Incorrect Service Selection: _____
_____
_____

Incorrect Primary Network Logon Settings:_____
_____
_____

Incorrect Computer Name or Workgroup Name: _____
_____
_____

Concept Question

Along with the integrated Help and Troubleshooting Files that come with the operating system, other resources are available. For issues not found in the Help and Troubleshooting Files database, there are other resources including the Windows 9x/NT/2000 Resource Kits and the various Internet Help/URLs.

List some web sites you have found that can be useful to the PC technician:

_____
_____
_____
_____
_____
_____
_____
_____

Additional Notes

_____

_____

_____

_____

_____

_____

_____

_____

_____

_____

_____

_____

_____

_____

_____

_____

_____

_____

Labs and Worksheets

The following labs and worksheets are available in the *CISCO NETWORKING ACADEMY PROGRAM IT Essentials I: PC Hardware and Software Lab Companion* and as part of the online curriculum. Labs and worksheets are an excellent tool that you can use to help reinforce the material covered in this chapter.

Labs

13.7.4 Booting into Safe Mode
13.7.5 Using the Windows 2000 Recovery Console
13.9.3 Windows Registry Backup and Recovery

Worksheets

13.4.5 Troubleshooting Software

A+ Exam Review Questions

The following are review questions for the A+ exam. Answers are found in Appendix A.

1.   What are the three things that make a successful technician?
    a.   Communication, local employees, smart dresser
    b.   Communication skills, technical skills, troubleshooting skills
    c.   Sense of humor, large inventory of parts, resource kits
    d.   Location, location, location

2.   When there is a problem with an end user's computer, you should note all of the following except?
    a.   When the problem occurred
    b.   If the problem occurs often
    c.   If the problem can be resolved by rebooting
    d.   The user's knowledge of computers

3.   To isolate the computer's problem during the troubleshooting process, you would do all the following except?
    a.   Reproduce the problem
    b.   Classify the problem
    c.   Reconfirm the problem
    d.   Remove all the internal components before doing anything else

4.   What is the MS-DOS based automated memory optimizer called?
    a.   MEM
    b.   Memmaker
    c.   REM
    d.   MSD

5.   Which key is pressed to skip Autoexec.bat and Config.sys when the message *Starting MS-DOS* displays?
    a.   F5
    b.   F6
    c.   F7
    d.   F8

6. Which of the following can recover files from damaged disks?
   a. Recover and FDISK
   b. Recover and Unformat
   c. Scandisk and Unformat
   d. Scandisk and Unformat
   e. Scandisk and Chkdsk

7. If you have Scandisk, you do not need to run?
   a. Fomat
   b. Chkdsk
   c. Fdisk
   d. Volume

8. Which utility can increase access speed by rearranging files and directories on the hard drive?
   a. Sort
   b. Scandisk
   c. Defrag
   d. Format

9. An *insufficient memory to run this application* error displays. What should you do?
   a. Install a hard drive with more empty space
   b. Increase the size of your swap file
   c. Buy more ROM chips
   d. Buy a new computer

10. Which of the following software problems will not corrupt files?
    a. Faulty hard drive
    b. Downloading problems
    c. Getting bad writes during a copy
    d. Defrag program problems

11. What is the most common symptom of a corrupt file?
    a. Overheating
    b. Inconsistent lock-ups
    c. Consistent lock-ups
    d. Unable to start computer

12. How do you access the Registry from Start > Run?

   a. Registry

   b. Regedit

   c. Sysedit

   d. System

13. What is the first thing to run if a computer locks up?

   a. Registry

   b. Scandisk

   c. Format

   d. Unlock

14. Why does a GPF occur?

   a. The hard disk cannot store any more data

   b. An application is using too many system resources

   c. An application is trying to write to a memory space occupied by another application

   d. A memory module in the computer has gone bad

15. What causes a page fault in Windows 98?

   a. Device drivers that are corrupt

   b. Applications that are poorly written

   c. Hard drives that are faulty

   d. All of the above

16. A NIC was working fine, but now it is causing connectivity problems. What do you check first?

   a. Just install a new NIC

   b. Upgrade the NIC driver

   c. Contact the vendor for any updates and patches

   d. Check to verify the NIC is installed and seated properly

17. Which two files do not load in Safe Mode?

   a. Autoexec.bat and Config.sys

   b. System.ini and Autoexec.bat

   c. Config.sys and Memmaker

   d. Autoexec.ini and Memmaker

18. The resource window for a device in the Device Manager displays the following, except?

    a.   IRQ

    b.   I/O address

    c.   Settings button

    d.   Delete settings button

19. The best utility to determine whether a specific IP address is accessible is?

    a.   Tracert.exe

    b.   Winipcfg.exe

    c.   Ping.exe

    d.   Netstat.com

20. Utility that traces a packet from the computer to an Internet host is?

    a.   Tracert.exe

    b.   Winipcfg.exe

    c.   Ping.exe

    d.   Netstat.com

Appendix A

Answers to A+ Exam Review Questions

Chapter 1

1. b
2. c
3. a
4. c
5. a
6. c
7. d
8. c
9. b
10. d
11. d
12. b
13. c
14. d
15. a
16. a
17. c
18. a
19. a
20. b

Chapter 2

1. a
2. c
3. b
4. b
5. c
6. c
7. b
8. d
9. b
10. c
11. a
12. d
13. b
14. a
15. c
16. b
17. a
18. d
19. a
20. b
21. d
22. c
23. c
24. d
25. a

Chapter 3

1. b
2. d
3. a
4. b
5. c
6. b
7. c
8. a
9. c
10. d
11. b
12. d
13. c
14. d
15. c
16. b
17. c
18. b
19. d
20. d
21. c
22. c
23. d
24. a
25. d

Chapter 4

1. c
2. c
3. b
4. a
5. c
6. a

7. d

8. b

9. c

10. d

11. a

12. d

13. d

14. b

15. d

16. d

17. c

18. b

19. d

20. a

21. b

22. d

23. a

24. a

25. c

Chapter 5

1. c

2. a

3. b

4. c

5. a

6. d

7. a

8. c

9. b

10. b

11. d

12. d

13. b

14. a

15. b

16. b

17. c

18. a

19. b

20. b

21. d

22. b

23. b

24. c

25. b

Chapter 6

1. c

2. a

3. d

4. a

5. b

6. a

7. c

8. b

9. a

10. c

11. d

12. c

13. a

14. b

15. d

16. b

17. a

18. c

19. a

20. c

Chapter 7

1. d

2. b

3. a

4. c

5. d

6. b

7. a

8. c

9. d

10. a

11. c

12. a

13. d

14. a

15. b

16. a

17. c

18. a

19. b

20. c

Chapter 8

1. d

2. a

3. c

4. b

5.   c
6.   a
7.   d
8.   b
9.   a
10.   c
11.   a
12.   c
13.   a
14.   d
15.   b
16.   a
17.   d
18.   b
19.   a
20.   c

Chapter 9

1.   c
2.   b
3.   b
4.   d
5.   d
6.   b
7.   a
8.   c
9.   b
10.   b
11.   d
12.   b
13.   c
14.   b

15.   d
16.   c
17.   a
18.   b
19.   d
20.   a
21.   d
22.   c
23.   a
24.   b
25.   d

Chapter 10

1.   c
2.   a
3.   d
4.   d
5.   b
6.   c
7.   a
8.   b
9.   b
10.   b
11.   a
12.   b
13.   a
14.   b
15.   b
16.   b
17.   c
18.   a
19.   b

20.   a

Chapter 11

1.   c
2.   a
3.   c
4.   b
5.   a
6.   a
7.   c
8.   b
9.   a
10.   d
11.   d
12.   a
13.   c
14.   b
15.   b
16.   a
17.   c
18.   a
19.   c
20.   d

Chapter 12

1.   d
2.   b
3.   a
4.   c
5.   d
6.   b
7.   a

8.	d		18.	d
9.	d		19.	c
10.	a		20.	a
11.	b			
12.	d			
13.	a			
14.	d			
15.	a			
16.	b			
17.	d			
18.	c			
19.	b			
20.	d			

Chapter 13

1. b
2. d
3. d
4. b
5. a
6. e
7. b
8. c
9. b
10. a
11. c
12. b
13. b
14. c
15. d
16. d
17. a

Appendix B

Math for the Digital Age

The more digital the world becomes, the more important it is to understand the basic function of digital systems. How do computers work at the most fundamental level? What is going on at the core of a computer that makes it perform a certain way? The answer is that it all comes down to 0s and 1s.

Boolean Logic Gates: AND, OR, NOT, NOR, XOR

The mathematics of logic was developed by English mathematician George Boole in the mid-19th century. Its rules govern logical functions (true/false).

Computers are built from various types of electronic circuits. These circuits depend on what are called AND, OR, NOT, and NOR logic gates. These gates are characterized by how they respond to input signals. The X and Y represent inputs, and the F represents output. Think of 0 as representing off and 1 as representing on.

AND   **OR**

inputs   output   inputs   output

NOR

NOT

The following truth tables allow a compact way to represent these boolean operations:

OR	0	1
0	0	1
1	1	1

AND	0	1
0	0	0
1	0	1

NOR	0	1
0	1	0
1	0	0

Decimal

The decimal, or Base 10, number system is used every day for doing math (counting change, measuring, telling time, and so on). The decimal number system uses 10 digits: 0, 1, 2, 3, 4, 5, 6, 7, 8, and 9.

It is useful to think in terms of powers of 10 (10^0, 10^1, 10^2, and so on) in relation to a decimal number. When focusing on the actual value of a decimal number, use the expanded form of the powers (1, 10, 100, and so on). It helps to keep track by using tables.

The Base 10 number 23,605 as it relates to the powers of 10 is shown in the table below:

10^4	10^3	10^2	10^1	10^0	Powers of 10
10,000	1,000	100	10	1	Expanded powers of 10
2	3	6	0	5	— **Expressed as power of 10**

The binary, or Base 2, number system uses two digits to express all numerical quantities. The only digits used in the binary number system are 0 and 1. An example of a binary number is 1001110101000110100101.

One important thing to remember is the role of the digit 0. Every number system uses the digit 0. However, whenever the digit 0 appears on the left side of a string of digits, it can be removed without changing the string value. For example, in Base 10, 02947 equals 2947. In Base 2, 0001001101 equals 1001101. Sometimes people include 0s on the left side of a number to emphasize places that would otherwise not be represented.

Another important concept when working with binary numbers is the powers of numbers. 2^0 and 2^3 are examples of numbers represented by powers. To describe these examples, say two to the zero and two to the three. Their values are the following: $2^0 = 1$, $2^1 = 2$, $2^2 = 2 \times 2 = 4$, $2^3 = 2 \times 2 \times 2 = 8$. Obviously, there is a pattern. The power is the number of 2s that need to be multiplied together. A common mistake is to confuse taking powers with simple multiplication: 2^4 is not equal to 2 x 4 = 8, instead it is equal to 2 x 2 x 2 x 2 = 16.

In Base 10, powers of ten are used. For example, 23605 in Base 10 means:

2 x 10000 + 3 x 1,000 + 6 x 100 + 0 x 10 + 5 x 1.

NOTE $10^0 = 1$, $10^1 = 10$, $10^2 = 100$, $10^3 = 1,000$, and $10^4 = 10,000$.

CAUTION Although 0 x 10 = 0, do not leave it out of the above equation. If it is not left out, the base 10 places all shift to the right, which gives the number 2,365 = 2 x 1,000 + 3 x 100 + 6 x 10 + 5 x 1 instead of 23605. Although a 0 within a number should never be ignored, ignoring or adding 0s to the beginning of numbers has no effect on their value. For instance, 23605 can be expressed as 0023605.

It is useful to think in terms of powers of 10 (10^0, 10^1, 10^2, and so on) in relation to a decimal number. When focusing on the actual value of a decimal number, use the expanded form of the powers (1, 10, 100, and so on). It helps to keep track by using tables. In the table above, see the Base 10 number 23605 as it relates to the powers of 10.

Binary

Binary means two. It is the principle behind digital computers. All input to the computer is converted into binary numbers made up of the two digits 0 and 1 (bits).

The table below can be used to convert the binary number 10010001 into decimal, as follows:

10010001 = 1 * 128 + 0 * 64 + 0 * 32 + 1 * 16 + 0 * 8 + 0 * 4 + 0 * 2 + 1 * 1 = 128 + 16 + 1 = 145

2^7	2^6	2^5	2^4	2^3	2^2	2^1	2^0	Powers of 2
128	64	32	16	8	4	2	1	Powers of 2 in decimal
1	0	0	1	0	0	0	1	Digits
								Expressed as a power of 2

The same method is used with binary numbers and powers of 2. Look at the binary number 10010001. The table above can be used to convert the binary number 10010001 into decimal as follows:

10010001 =

1 x 128 +

0 x 64 +

0 x 32 +

1 x 16 +

0 x 8 +

$0 \times 4 +$

$0 \times 2 +$

$1 \times 1 =$

$128 + 16 + 1 = 145$

This is one of the ways to convert a binary number into a decimal number.

Decimal to Binary Conversion

There is usually more than one way to solve a math problem, and decimal to binary conversion is no exception. One method is explored here, but feel free to use another method if it is easier.

The table below shows conversion to a binary number:

2^6	2^5	2^4	2^3	2^2	2^1	2^0
64	32	16	8	4	2	1
0	1	0	0	0	1	1

To convert a decimal number to binary, the idea is to first find the biggest power of 2 that will fit into the decimal number. Consider the decimal number 35. Looking at the chart above, what is the greatest power of 2 that fits into 35? Starting with the largest number, 2^6, or 64 is greater than 35. Place a 0 in that column.

The next largest number, 2^5, or 32, is smaller than 35. Place a 1 in that column. Now, calculate how much is left over by subtracting 32 from 35. The result is 3.

Next, ask if 16 (the next lower power of 2) fits into 3. Because it does not, a 0 is placed in that column.

The value of the next number is 8, which is larger than 3, so a 0 is placed in that column.

The next value is 4, which is still larger than 3, so it too receives a 0.

The next value is 2, which is smaller than 3. Because 2 fits into 3, place a 1 in that column. Now subtract 2 from 3, which results in 1.

The last number's value is 1, which fits in the remaining number left. Thus, place a 1 in the last column.

The binary equivalent of the decimal number 35 is 0100011. Ignoring the first 0, the binary number can be written as 100011.

This method works for any decimal number. Consider the decimal number 1 million. What's the biggest power of 2 that fits in the decimal number 1,000,000? $2^{19} = 524,288$ and $2^{20} = 1,048,576$, so 2^{19} is the largest power of 2 that fits into 1,000,000. Continuing with the procedure described above, determine that the decimal number 1 million is equal to the binary number 11110100001001000000.

This technique can rapidly become clumsy, when dealing with large numbers.

The Base 16 (Hexadecimal) Number System

The Base 16, or hexadecimal, number system is used frequently when working with computersbecause it can represent binary numbers in a more readable form. The computer performs computations in binary, but there are several instances when a computer's binary output is expressed in hexadecimal to make it easier to read.

The table below shows a base 16 conversion.

16^5	16^4	16^3	16^2	16^1	16^0	Powers of 16
1,048,576	65,536	4096	256	16	1	Powers of 16 in decimal
0	B	2	3	C	F	Digits

The most common way for computers and software to express hexadecimal output is using 0x in front of the hexadecimal number. Whenever 0x is seen, the number that follows is a hexadecimal number. For example, 0x1234 means 1234 in Base 16.

Base 16 uses 16 characters to express numerical quantities. These characters are 0, 1, 2, 3, 4, 5, 6, 7, 8, 9, A, B, C, D, E, and F. An A represents the decimal number 10, B represents 11, C represents 12, D represents 13, E represents 14, and F represents 15. Examples of hexadecimal numbers are 2A5F, 99901, FFFFFFFF, and EBACD3. A number such as B23CF (hexadecimal) = 730,063 (decimal).

The traditional conversion between decimal and hexadecimal is outside the scope of this course. However, later in this chapter, some shortcuts for conversion to any base, including decimal and hexadecimal, will be discussed

Binary to Hexadecimal Conversion

Binary to hexadecimal conversion is fairly straightforward. First observe that 1111 in binary is F in hexadecimal. Also, 11111111 in binary is FF in hexadecimal. Without going into a mathematical proof, one fact that is useful when working with these two number systems is that one hexadecimal character requires 4 bits, or 4 binary digits, to be represented in binary. A bit is simply a binary digit. Used in the binary numbering system, it can be 0 or 1.

To convert a binary number to hexadecimal, group the number into groups of four bits at a time, starting from the right. Then convert each group of four bits into hexadecimal, thus producing a hexadecimal equivalent to the original binary number.

The table below shows binary to hexadecimal conversion.

Binary	Hexadecimal
0000	0
0001	1
0010	2
0011	3
0100	4
0101	5
0110	6
0111	7
1000	8
1001	9
1010	A
1011	B
1100	C
1101	D
1110	E
1111	F

Take, for example, the binary number 11110111001100010000. Breaking it down into groups of four bits would equal 1111 0111 0011 0001 0000. This binary number is equivalent to F7310 in hexadecimal (a much easier number to read).

As another example, the binary number 111101 is grouped as 11 1101 or, when padded with 0s, 0011 1101. Thus, the hexadecimal equivalent is 3D.

Hexadecimal to Binary Conversion

Converting numbers from hexadecimal to binary is really just the reverse method of the previous section. Take each individual hexadecimal digit and convert it to binary, and string together the solution. However, be careful to pad each binary representation with 0s to fill up four binary places for each hexadecimal digit, as shown in the table above. For example, take the hexadecimal number FE27. F is 1111, E is 1110, 2 is 10 or 0010, and 7 is 0111. So, in binary, the answer is 1111 1110 0010 0111, or 1111111000100111.

The table below shows hexadecimal to binary conversion.

Hexadecimal	Binary
0	0000
1	0001
2	0010
3	0011
4	0100
5	0101
6	0110
7	0111
8	1000
9	1001
A	1010
B	1011
C	1100
D	1101
E	1110
F	1111

Converting to Any Base

Most people already know how to do many number conversions. For instance, when converting inches to yards, first divide the number of inches by 12 to get the number of feet. The remainder is the number of inches left. Next divide the number of feet by 3 to get the number of yards. The remainder is the number of feet left. These same techniques are used for converting numbers to other bases.

If converting from decimal (the normal base) to octal, Base 8 (known here as the foreign base) for example, divide by 8 (the foreign base) successively and keep track of the remainders starting from the least significant remainder.

Take the number 1234 in decimal and convert it to octal.

$$1234 / 8 = 154 \text{ R } 2$$

$$154 / 8 = 19 \text{ R } 2$$

$$19 / 8 = 2 \text{ R } 3$$

$$2 / 8 = 0 \text{ R } 2$$

The result is 2322 in octal.

To convert back again, multiply a running total by 8 and add each digit successively starting with the most significant number.

$$2 * 8 = 16$$

$$16 + 3 = 19$$

$$19 * 8 = 152$$

$$152 + 2 = 154$$

$$154 * 8 = 1232$$

$$1232 + 2 = 1234$$

Similar techniques can be used to convert to and from any base just by dividing or multiplying by the foreign base.

However, binary is unique in that odd and even can determine 1s and 0s without recording the remainders. Given the same number that we used above, 1234, determine the binary equivalent simply by dividing it by 2 successively. The bit is determined by the odd and evenness of the result. If the result is even, the bit associated with it is 0. If the result is odd, the binary digit associated with it is 1.

1234 is even record a 0 in the least significant position.

1234/2 = 617 is odd record a 1 in the next most significant position (10)

617/2 = 308 is even (010)

308/2 = 154 is even (0010)

154/2 = 77 is odd (10010)

77/2 = 38 is even (010010)

38/2 = 19 is odd (1010010)

19/2 = 9 is odd (11010010)

9/2 = 4 is even (011010010)

4/2 = 2 is even (0011010010)

2/2 = 1 is odd (10011010010)

With practice, the running dividend can be mastered and the binary can be written quickly.

Just as a hexadecimal digit is a group of four bits, an octal is a group of three digits. Group the above number into groups of three starting at the right:

010,011,010,010 = 2322 octal

For hex, group by four bits:

0100,1101,0010 = 4D2 hexadecimal or 0x4D2

This is a quick and easy method to convert to any base.

Appendix C

Safety Requirements and Organization

Safety precautions are emphasized and reviewed to keep the technician safe and to protect expensive computer components. The lab safety principals must be followed and the lab safety agreement should be signed before beginning the assembly process.

Basic Lab Safety Principals

The following are the basic lab safety principals that must be followed when handling computer components:

- Use an anti-static mat and grounding wrist strap or grounding wrist strap only.
- Use anti-static bags to store and move computer components. Do not put more than one component in each bag, as stacking them can cause some of the components to become loose or broken.
- Do not remove or install components while the computer is on. If there has been a mistake in wiring or component installation, turn the computer off and unplug it before replacing the cable or component.
- Ground yourself often to prevent static charges from building up. Touch a piece of bare metal on the chassis or power supply.
- Work on a bare floor, if possible, as carpets can build up static charges.
- Hold cards by the edges. Avoid touching chips or the edge connectors on the expansion cards.
- Do not touch chips or expansion boards with a magnetized screwdriver.
- Always turn off the computer before moving it. This is to protect the hard drive, which is always spinning when the computer is turned on.
- Keep computer disks away from magnetic fields, heat, and cold.
- When laying components down, put them on top of an anti-static bag or mat. Never place a circuit board of any kind onto a conductive surface, especially a metal foil. The lithium and nickel cadmium (NiCad) batteries used on boards can short out.
- Do not use a pencil or metal tipped instrument to change DIP switches or touch or probe components. The graphite in the pencil is conductive and could easily cause damage.
- Do not allow anyone who is not properly grounded to touch or hand off computer components. This is true even when working with a lab partner. When passing components, always touch hands first to neutralize any charges.
- Do not allow food or drink in the work area.
- Keep the work area clean and orderly. When finished with a tool or component, put it back into its proper place.

Workspace Safety

The following is a list of guidelines that help create a safe, efficient work environment:

1. The workspace should be large enough to accommodate the system unit, the technician's tools, the testing equipment, and the electrostatic discharge (ESD) prevention equipment. Near the workbench, power outlets should be available to at least accommodate the system unit power and the power needs of other electrical devices.

2. The workspace should maintain a humidity level of between 20 percent - 50 percent to reduce the likelihood of ESD.

3. The workbench should be a nonconductive surface; additionally, it should have a flat, cleanable surface.

4. The workspace should be distant from areas of heavy electrical equipment or concentrations of electronics.

5. The workspace should be free of dust. Dust can contaminate the workspace, which causes premature damage to computer components. The work area should have a filtered air system to reduce dust and contaminants.

6. Lighting should be adequate to see small details. Two different illumination forms are preferred: an adjustable lamp with a shade, and fluorescent lighting.

7. Extreme variations of temperature can affect computer components. Temperatures should be maintained so that they are consistent with the specifications of the components.

8. Properly grounded AC electrical current is essential. Power outlets should be tested with an outlet tester for proper grounding.

Organizational Aids

The following are organizational aids that every IT technician should have in the workspace:

- A parts organizer to keep track of small parts such as screws and connectors
- Adhesive or masking tape to make labels that identify parts
- A small notebook to keep track of assembly and troubleshooting steps
- A place for quick references and detailed troubleshooting guides
- A clipboard for paperwork

Lab Safety Agreement

Before repairing any electronic device, know the hazards and safety factors. Use extreme care and follow these safety procedures at all times. Read and sign this agreement.

1.   Remove all jewelry.

2.   Always unplug the power cord before removing or reinstalling any electrical component or circuit board, or when performing maintenance on electrical equipment.

3.   Do not touch any exposed circuit with power applied.

4.   Only have power applied when taking voltage measurements or waveforms.

5.   Insert test probes with one hand only. Do not insert probes with both hands. Keeping one hand behind your back or under the test bench reduces the chance of fatal electrocution. This is referred to as the one-hand rule.

6.   Do not leave any objects loose on the equipment, such as screws, nuts, or washers. They can fall into the equipment.

7.   Before handling or replacing IC processors, properly ground yourself by touching the outside metal of the equipment and by using an anti-static wrist strap that is connected to the chassis. Make sure that the equipment is grounded prior to removing its case. This reduces ESD damage.

8.   Do not troubleshoot electronic equipment without having appropriate documentation, unless instructor approval is given.

9.   Never solder any connection with the power on.

10.   After soldering, look for possible solder splashes, cold solder joints, or damaged insulation.

11.   Always maintain a clean and safe work area.

12.   Take your time.

13.   Be certain about what you are going to do. If you are unsure about a procedure, ask for help.

14.   IF IN DOUBT, DON'T TOUCH IT!

15.   Know the location of fire extinguishers, all fire evacuation procedures, safety/First Aid kit locations and emergency phone numbers in class.

16.   Shoes, shirt, and long pants are required when soldering and working on equipment.

STUDENT ACKNOWLEDGMENT

I have read and understand this document.

_____   _____

Student Signature   Print Name   Date

Sample Inventory Checklist

The first step in the computer assembly process is to get organized. All the components used to assemble a computer should be listed on an inventory. The inventory should be updated as the system is changed or updated.

Computer Identification

Name: _____

Number: _____

Computer Case

Manufacturer: _____

Type: (Mini, Midi, Full, Desktop) _____

Number of:

3.5-inch bays _____

5.25-inch bays _____

Motherboard

Manufacturer: _____   Model: _____

Bus Speed _____MHz _____

Form Factor:

▲ AT

▲ ATX

Chipset Manufacturer:_____

Model: _____

BIOS Manufacturer:_____

Version: _____

Does the CPU use a socket or a slot? _____

How many CPU sockets/slots are there?_____

How many ISA slots are there? _____

How many PCI slots are there? _____

How many EIDE connectors are there?_____

How many floppy connectors are there? _____

How many serial ports are there? _____

How many parallel ports are there? _____

Is there an AGP slot? _____

How many USB ports are there? _____

How many other ports or slots are there? _____

What kind(s) are they? _____

CPU

Manufacturer: _____

Model: _____

Speed: _____MHz _____

Memory

30-pin SIMMs _____

72-pin SIMMs _____

168-pin DIMMs _____

160 pin RIMMs _____

184-pin RIMMs _____

Other: _____

How many memory slots are there? _____

What is the fastest type of memory supported? _____

What is the maximum memory supported? _____

Hard Drive

Manufacturer: _____

Model: _____

Size: _____

Cylinders: _____

Heads: _____

SPT: _____

Interface Type:

▲ IDE

▲ SCSI

CD-ROM

Manufacturer: _____

Model: _____

Speed: _____

Interface Type:

▲ IDE

▲ SCSI

CD-ROM RW

Manufacturer: _____

Model: _____

Speed: _____

Interface Type:

▲ IDE

▲ SCSI

DVD Drive

Manufacturer: _____

Model: _____

Speed: _____

Interface Type:

▲ IDE

▲ SCSI

Floppy Disk Drive

Manufacturer: _____

Monitor

Manufacturer: _____

Model Number: _____

Monitor Size: _____

Video Card

Manufacturer: _____

Model: _____

Memory: _____   MB   _____

- ISA
- PCI
- On Board
- AGP

Sound Card

Manufacturer: _____

Model: _____

- ISA
- PCI
- On Board

Mouse

- PS/2
- Serial
- USB

Keyboard

Connector:

- 5-pin DIN
- 6-pin mini-DIN
- USB

Make sure that it matches the connector on your motherboard.

Power Supply:

- AT
- ATX
- Other: _____

Power Supply Wattage: _____

Tape Backup

Manufacturer: _____

Model: _____

Scanner

Manufacturer: _____   Model: _____

Speakers

Manufacturer: _____

Model: _____

Additional Information

_____
_____
_____
_____
_____
_____
_____
_____
_____
_____

Assembly Check List

After all the components and parts have been installed in the case, it is time to complete the PC assembly process. Before closing the computer case, review the following checklist:

_____   Are there any loose screws in the computer case?

_____   Have all tools been removed from the computer case?

_____   Is the voltage selector switch in the correct position?

_____   Is the CPU seated completely?

_____   Is the fan secured?

_____   Is the fan plugged in?

_____   Is the memory in the correct slot, and is it fully seated?

_____   Are all the drives in their correct position and secure to the chassis?

_____   Are the ribbon cables fully seated and connected to the correct drives?

_____   Is the audio cable connected to the CD-ROM drive correctly?

_____   Is the ATX 1 power cable in the right position and has it been latched down?